My Reflec
England

Charmiene Maxwell-Batten

Charmiene in Cornwall

My Reflections of England

Charmiene Maxwell-Batten

Copyright

Charmiene Maxwell-Batten
Is the author of:

Life, Love and Loss in Switzerland

My Reflections of America

My Reflections of India and Thailand

Araminta's Message

My Reflections of Childhood

Reflections of a Housekeeper

A Medley of Musings and Reflections

A Collage of Reflections
A Collage of Reflections Volume 2

One More Chance

Exeter Cathedral in Devon

Historical cottage in Lyme Regis Dorset

Contents

Acknowledgements

Thank you to all the people and incidents that have been inspirational in writing this book. I want to thank my husband Gaylan LeRoy Mills, for the love and support he gives me. Thank you to Sheila Lyon for your forthright candor in my editing process. Gratitude to Atmo Ram (Scott Leland) for giving me the initial encouragement and opportunity to write and for the use of your beautiful Haikus. Thank you to my three brothers, Jonny, Justin and Dominic Maxwell-Batten, for being my family.

To Diana Fairbank in Washington USA, Peggy Seppelt in Dresden Germany and Peter Scott in Devon England for helping me convert files to PDF during the earlier stages of - publishing. Thank you to Laura Redmond and David W. Morin Jr. for your help in formatting my books for EPUB.

Seagull in Lyme Regis

Dedication

This book is dedicated to the village of Topsham in Devon,

where my family live.

Where boats are anchored in the peaceful Estuary

and local pubs like

The Globe, *The Passage*,

The Lighter Inn and *The Bridge Inn*

provide moments of friendly respite.

Cemetery in Topsham.
Beautiful pink cherry blossom at the entrance
This is where the bodies of my parents' lie in rest

Introduction

My narratives began in 1991 after purchasing a computer. Through the creative expression of authoring, I find myself communicating an array of thoughts, emotions and observable occurrences. Immersed in a cocoon with an ever-faithful laptop, I quietly reflect on my life, and our, shared human existence.

Characters described in this book are a little older now and some have passed on. My observations of human nature and incidents are real, though the identities of a few individuals have been replaced with fictitious names in order to preserve privacy. *'Rita and Paddy'* and several others have retained their true names; I couldn't imagine finding alternative representations for so many caring and distinctive people.

I begin with the chapter *'Starlings'* because it touches on the historic village of Topsham in Devon where my family now live; we even have a family tree going back to Sir John Follett in eighteenth century Topsham. Anyone who lives in Topsham will be familiar with the captivating sunsets enveloping this quiet estuary night after night.

The last few chapters are filled with memories of my mother.

Having traveled and lived in other countries, my personality has evolved into a mosaic of colorful differences originating from the various lands that I call home. Even though an accent and heritage with a paternal family tree going back to the eleventh century renders a really British character, I've spent years and years in other countries.

My mother too, though born in Mexico City had undeniably English parents. Her grandparents emigrated to Mexico from Europe and throughout my life I heard fragmented and mysterious stories about the Austrian upheaval of the aristocracy in the early 20th Century when a member of Mum's family fled to South America. Numerous other Europeans enjoyed a lavish lifestyle in that country until the latest political leader ejected them.

Great grandfather John Maxwell-Batten was born in Almora, India where his father was a British military officer in the Bengali civil service. My *other* great grandfather Sabine Baring-Gould, toured all over Europe including a momentous and pioneering journey through Iceland, only coming home to minister solicitously to his large congregation, to write numerous intriguing books, procreate and watch his beloved children grow up. Perhaps it is 'in my blood' to travel!

Though a collective interest in the human spirit is timeless I realize that these narratives *are* personal. Hopefully the subjective nature of my interpretation will also strike an inspirational chord in the reader. We may be 'Islands' and uniquely different - at the same time we all have a shared capacity to feel and respond to the universality of life.

"Art is the only way to run away,
without leaving home"

Twyla Tharp

Starlings

Topsham was an old smuggling village in days gone by, and still today it's filled with an interesting and mysterious past.

Relaxing on the stonewall overlooking the Estuary, we (Scott and myself) watched the starlings gather on summer evenings. After purchasing tea and beer from the well-known Lighter Inn nearby we carried our beverages over to the algae covered sea wall.

We sipped our drinks as the day softly dissolved into the soft horizon and twilight descended on the quiet Estuary. Life was good.

Dramatic sunsets inevitably urged us there night after night and the appearance of starlings was an extra and much appreciated prize. They flew in front of a setting sun covering the burning red sky with black dots, fluttering in unison while stretching and elongating. Suddenly crowding together in a black mass, only to elongate again like a rubber band, this visual concert was a synchronized movement in the sky's expanse. It was a vivid concert that held me spellbound for the entire evening.

Swans gliding up to the wall in their search for food imparted a contemplative setting. Boats were being moored up for the night after chugging in from the day's jaunt. I loved those peaceful activities in the dusky finale of a day.

When the sky took on its apricot and rosy hues, the starlings continued circling the vicinity while all the time smaller groups from the surrounding area joined them, quickly merging in with the gathering. In the early evening they often sat on the brown tiled roof of the church nearby, waiting for their group to assemble.

Darker blue hues came looming in from the sky when the birds seemed to have finally gathered their troops and with one dramatic swoop, they crowded together and fell into the marshes. That was it!

Once settled, a noise must have disturbed them on one of those placid, summer evenings; they rose out of the marshes in an excited mass, circled around for a while, and as a unified throng, descended again for the night.

One may plausibly assume that this display night after night could become monotonous, yet it was always captivating; the natural rippling movement through the evening sky was mesmerizing. Nature offers an opportunity to be present in each new moment and to perceive the recurring enchantment through fresh eyes, always unique and always different. It's not surprising that artists come especially to this village on the Estuary to listen to the song of the evening, while soulful eyes and deftly moving hands, create a painting.

On one of those evenings an artist from Germany was sitting on the stonewall close by and while absorbed in her work, I glimpsed a sensation of colors and emotion on canvas. She later explained that she had been coming to this location for the past five years, and each year there was even more to express through the mysterious language of art.

I continue to look for the starlings whenever I visit Topsham, because it signifies a place where I found and still find peace. Now, walking to that evocative place on the wall, I am bathed in a wave of nostalgia and many good memories.

The Red Arrows

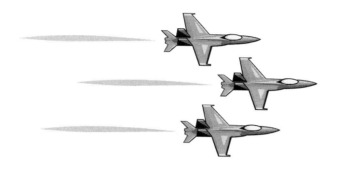

It was one of those consequential moments, so perfectly orchestrated in order to encounter a marvel.

While nonchalantly driving around on this warm and sunny afternoon during a hot summer in 1995, our only goal was to enjoy the picturesque scenery in Devon. Just above the small seaside town, crowds were gathering on a hill whilst eagerly looking at the bay ahead.

An added stroke of luck was the parking space surprisingly available by the granite wall. Stepping out and easily slipping into an ideal gap in the multitude of onlookers, we found ourselves gazing at the horizon with all the other spectators. I saw a number of varying sized boats anchored quietly in the cove; it must be a boat show, I thought.

Out of nowhere six red planes darted in front of us, so vividly close that the sheer brilliance of movement took me aback. The soft blue sky provided a flawless stage for a performance that was to enthrall and impress the crowds for an entire hour. One of life's rare and unexpected gifts was tossed upon me in that moment in time, as the planes dashed and danced around the sky; colors were streaming from the engines painting the sky with red and blue streaks. I could only gaze in awe at the acrobats and pirouettes performed by these machines. The pilots seemed primed with exactness and exuberance, allowing their souls to soar with their machines while at the same time maintaining focus and precision. I could *feel* the pilots' exhilaration in this display of brilliance.

Scott had been a Naval Officer in San Diego California, Miramar where the movie Top Gun was filmed and where the authentic Top Gun headquarters were located. He had on many occasions seen the American fighter pilots in practice. I'd seen the Blue Angels perform while living in Alaska. In spite of the stirring impressions of our earlier experience, this presentation by the Red Arrows was utterly breathtaking.

Neither lengthy plans nor financial exchanges had led to this occasion, it was an encounter born of freedom and the elements of surprise. Driving away from this little town we were stunned to see that masses of people had gathered at the seafront; crowds that seemed like thousands of ants milling around the holiday resort of Dawlish.

Whenever life seems tough, brutal and even bleak, I shall try to remember that it can be inspirational and dazzling. I never cease to be amazed at mankind's ability to reach far beyond the physical world in an effort to convey the heights of our soaring spirit. I believe those pilots expressed an inner freedom in the magnificence of their performance. They uplifted me that day.

I don't believe that humans can truly imitate or copy nature but in this instance the acrobatic dance of these machines was comparable to the intrinsic beauty of a flock of birds in lively flight where both expressed a ballet of synchronized movement. But then the pilots were not trying to imitate, they were merely being themselves.

A chance encounter, not to be missed!

Photo by Marjorie Wallace

*"Written into every atom and molecule
of our body,
is the history of the Universe"*

Brian Edward Cox.
Physicist and Humanist

24

A Visit to a Graveyard

What is it about English graveyards that seem to encourage an abundance of tales, narratives and mysteries relating to the supernatural? My hunch is that our damp English churches and the surrounding land allocated to the aged moss-covered gravestones have a distinctive charm that arouses ghostly reflections. Having traveled a great deal, I treasure the unique character of English churchyards with graves that have no apparent uniformity to them.

My Swiss husband at that time, who was a keen photographer in the 1970's, seemed fascinated by these unkempt masterpieces of English tradition. He proceeded to photograph them in their myriad and mist shrouded forms; the only thing they had in common, he said, was their eccentricity. After growing up in Switzerland where order and tidiness is undoubtedly part of an ingrained culture, this visual portrayal must have been enchantingly inconsistent. By utilizing each plot efficiently, graveyards in Switzerland are not only neatly placed, but are planned with precision and regularity in mind. They're well taken care of and there is always space for a fresh grave. After thirty years, 'old' graves are eliminated in order to make space for 'new' ones. It's hard to find ageing moss-covered graves there.

I came across an intriguing graveyard high up in the Swiss mountains, where orderly rows with clearly defined pictures of deceased people were deftly and lovingly placed on gravestones. It was uncanny and I hadn't seen anything like it until now. In a familiar kind of way, those aged and dilapidated foggy cemeteries in England were reassuring, whereas this neat line of shiny brass-polished graves displaying vivid pictures of a dead person, seemed eerie.

While strolling through a church near London in the early nineties, I was surprised that a mere handful of discernible older graves were visible. Some were four hundred and fifty years old but I had expected to see many more antiquated memorials as a natural heritage of an English church. I walked with someone who had lost his wife eighteen years before, and while visiting his wife's place of rest, the seventy-five year old man explained that there was lack of space now in London. Corpses were now cremated instead of being buried. Ashes were placed in one small and meager patch of grass with no flowers to indicate the numerous visits that had evidently taken place. His wife's ashes were mingled with many others who had died over the past eighteen years. An individual and 'special spot' for a grieving person was missing - instead they were crowded together on one small piece of grass.

That day I knew that the actual significance of a grave was for those people still living. In fact a woman who had lost her husband seven months before, expressed this exact sentiment: *"I'm going to sit with Ian for a while."*

She voiced a poignant longing to place a red rose where his ashes lay. Alas it was not permitted. Apparently flowers created clutter for someone to tidy up.

A shrine or memorial offers great comfort to a brokenhearted person who is often lonely in this physical world and needing to feel close to their departed loved one.

After my own baby daughter died, visiting her grave brought fresh pain and tears to my aching heart. It was nonetheless this very act of being there and standing in silence at her graveside that facilitated a recognition and the healing to cope with such a loss. I'm not sure that I would have been able to do this adequately at a patch of grass that could in no way be identified as my daughter's grave. At the time of writing this book, my daughter's grave is no longer there, which has caused an added sense of loss. Yes, her grave reached the thirty-year 'allowance' in Switzerland; now thirty-five years later, I deeply wish to re-visit her grave, but it's not possible.

Are English graves going from disorganized memorials of stone, rich in charm and character - to a barren patch of grass with no possibility of planting flowers?

The gentleman who had lost his wife eighteen years before, had very rarely in all those years been able to sit quietly or unaccompanied beside his wife's burial spot. Well-meaning people were frequently walking by and greeting him. Many others shared that exact same spot where their loved one had also been placed. It was not private. I was glad that I had that special spot allocated to the grave of my little daughter, even for only thirty years - and the space to experience in private and without intrusion, what I needed to feel. To plant a rose on her tiny grave and see it grow into blossom over the months, was vital in coping with my own grief.

The essence of my narrative is to hint at the significance of a graveside aimed specifically for the needs of those who've lost someone very dear. I'd miss the charm of traditional English Churchyards if they became obsolete and replaced by a small patch of grass with no sign of color. A seemingly impersonal patch of grass to which collectively, many have a claim.

The seventy-five year old gentleman had a stained glass window erected in the local church, which was dedicated to his wife; this beautiful pastel, mauve colored glass decoration was a symbol of his love. This was the shrine where he could sit in silence and feel that deep bond that they had shared, and as far as I could see, still share.

As our population continues to grow the space for these sizable shrines in our current environment is not unlimited; many people now genuinely wish to be cremated and indeed have their loved ones cremated. On a very personal level, the sight of that small meager and yes, barren patch was saddening particularly when recalling the graves I'd seen in Switzerland that were carpeted in sweet smelling flowers; though, I never did see a grave that was four hundred and fifty years old in Switzerland.

A Cafe

Hoping to warm my bones with a pot of hot tea in a warm toasty room, it was a cold wintry day in 1979 when walking into a café in downtown Exeter. Climbing up some rickety threadbare 'carpeted' stairs, my breath soared with each misty exhalation and was *still* making frosty smoke signals in the chilly café at the top of the stairs. Keeping a coat on while sipping the strong tea, I reminded myself that this *is* England. Had I been overly pampered during the last few years in Switzerland, where crispy weather outside is countered by the warmth and comfort of being indoors? The Swiss are very practical.

Heating systems in the English wintertime were never efficient; double-glazing was unheard of. Here I was back in Britain and watching my warm breath producing foggy patterns in a freezing room.

Since then, numerous avant-garde continental style and *warm* tearooms have emerged. I'm not sure whether I feel relieved or a bit sad now that this particular variety of run-down café is dying out. That dim and disheveled refuge struck me as being one of the few remaining characteristics of an English way of life. Older traditional tearooms where comfortable and grand living-room scenes, usually including a big log fireplace, still flourish as they always have done in this country. How much longer I wonder? They too are slowly being replaced by trendy hotel café /bars.

Though a bare and bleak setting is in no way alluring, I nevertheless feel a sentimental twinge of wistfulness at the loss of this rundown café and the thought that another trait of 'Englishness' may become extinct.

The contrast of that threadbare staircase and chilly setting instigates an immeasurable appreciation of soft armchairs, log fires and elegant surroundings. Two totally differing extremes in the world of tearooms in England provided an avenue of rest for everyone anytime - until the fashionable and continental style cafes appeared!

The Georgian Tearoom

Walking into one of our favourite tearooms in Topsham, Mum was excited at the thought of a deliciously decadent strawberry Pavlova! Already seated that day, in seemingly solemn clusters, were a few other patrons, who conveyed a quietly rigid demeanour. Their stern faces did not seem stress-free and I could almost hear their inward chatter.

Absorbed in our merry conversation, Mum, my nephew, and I were busy enjoying the edibles as much as one another's company. As time went on I became more aware of small groups of people in the room, some of whom seemed to be surreptitiously listening to our conversation. Our chitchat evidently caught their attention, yet an open display of interest or even curiosity in our lively chatter was unthinkable.

Whenever I looked in someone's direction, eyes would dart elsewhere, thereby maintaining a veneer of nonchalance which seemed crucial. I felt acutely aware of being in a small 'living-room' type ambience - with strangers.

People appeared to be straining to hear our conversation. Were they fully enjoying their own experience? Were they encroaching on ours? Perhaps we were a little too animated that day.

One of many pleasurable characteristics of an English tearoom impels a controlled manner of decorum accompanied by gracious conversation. Placid moments of sipping tea intermingled with melodious conversation or else some merry unobtrusive chatting over a cup of tea, gives people a chance to relax. I felt uncomfortable in this instant, where an atmosphere of rigidly hushed people appeared to be eavesdropping. A pretense at being hushed.

My mother very rarely allowed her childlike cheerfulness to be subdued; our strawberry pavlova and merry chatter was certainly a treasured opportunity. I would like to think that we brought a spark of brightness to the tearoom on that particular afternoon. The patrons may have been relieved when we left; perhaps we seemed a bit too vibrant.

We went back numerous times after. During summer months, chairs and tables were set in the pretty garden with charming tablecloths and china. A friendly atmosphere and cheery service gave mum so much enjoyment. Then after mum died, I went to this tearoom with dad – we sat for a couple of hours enjoying the food, peace and tranquillity of this lovely haven in Topsham. I enjoyed those moments with my parents.

.

"For small creatures such as we,
The vastness is bearable only through love"

Carl Sagan

The lovely Georgian tearoom

The Ice Cream

Nine year old Luke and Sam were given two English pounds cash to buy ice cream for themselves as well as for the five younger children on that hot sunny day in July. Luke's mother owned a small day-care center for children, often welcoming them as tiny babies when they were just a few weeks old. Parents' who had chosen to pursue successful careers entrusted their offspring to someone they had confidence in. They were happy children in this caring environment.

School holidays for Luke, Sam as well as all the other older children in the village enabled them to spend warm summer days camping or playing on the Estuary banks.

My sister anticipated that the money, two pounds, would be shared amongst all the children. Those were her instructions. It was certainly possible for everyone to enjoy their treat since the five little ones favored less costly 'milk lollies', the two older boys would have enough money left over to each buy a substantial treat for themselves. All for two pounds!

The two boys arrived back happily carrying their treats. Sam, a big smile on his face was clutching an enormous colorful ice cream covered in extravagant decorations, while joyfully exclaiming that he had spent a whole pound all on himself. Luke had bought six little milk lollies including his own with the remaining one-pound. He arrived back carrying all six.

Being aware of a world where adults may possess and acquire vast amounts of accoutrements and all too frequently exploit others to gain these ends, so as to be the proud owner of a 'big ice cream', I was saddened to see this avarice displayed in a nine year old child. Accumulating wealth while depleting land or polluting seas and oceans and leaving the remaining people with 'milk lollies', seems to be an achievement to aspire to. Who can grab the biggest ice cream - is this really a desire of humanity? Is it clever to take advantage of someone else and have miserly values been *learnt* or do they come naturally?

Sam, who thought he had been quick-witted, was delighted at his triumph.

The elevated qualities of altruism, kindness and perception seem to be revealed in human nature as early as nine years old and can magnify into adulthood. Luke, an intelligent child with big brown eyes, had clearly seen what Sam had pulled off, but chose not to engage or even comment on the incident. I wondered how Luke would mature into maturity; would he take a stand and speak out at injustice or would he himself acquiesce to the traits demonstrated by Sam?

Our collective journey into adulthood evolves from a kaleidoscope of experiences as well as an inherent and inborn personality. I was deeply touched by Luke's disinclination to rebuke or express disapproval of Sam, and perhaps in his unspoken wisdom, Luke knew that Sam was a neglected child who had not been showered with tender and authentic love. Luke's father was a kind and caring man who cared about others. I am sure this example rubbed off on Luke too.

"A Native American Grandfather talking to his young
grandson tells the boy he has two wolves inside him
struggling with each other.
The first is the wolf of peace, love and kindness.
The other wolf is fear, greed and hatred.
"Which wolf will win grandfather?" Asks the young boy
"Whichever one I feed" is the reply

Native American Proverb

Buying and Selling Freedom

We *are* free, aren't we - free to make choices?

Even though the outcome of our decisions clearly resides in a higher place and not in the control of our mortal hands, nevertheless hard earned wisdom and an acknowledgement of this undeniable truth does impart peace to those who recognize it.

Difficult circumstances, be they financial, emotional, spiritual, or otherwise convinces many that a state of personal limitation is evident and thus a craving for liberation on various levels is born. A yearning for the freedom to speak one's truth and 'find oneself' induces an intense search for genuine harmony. Once the quest is launched, there begins a dedicated spiritual journey towards the inner self. Attaining paradise or the state of 'Nirvana' can also be a human illusion. For many, it's an unwavering goal. Perhaps this true state of enlightenment is much closer and unpredicted than we realize.

Plenty of teachers, group leaders, therapists, spiritual advisors and psychics will offer 'paradise and liberation'. Pay some money and you can *have it;* it's evidently for sale. Sign up for the next program and there's invariably a follow-up program. The recently launched self-help and new age workshops flourish in response to a growing demand for the desire and hope of attaining 'Nirvana', which impels pursuing this path with commitment and anticipation.

It *is* a worthy craving and much less harmful than some habits, because it really supports the well-being of the body and may even resolve various emotional issues. Coping better within our society may be an added benefit. This particular urge and its thirst for fulfillment is admirable but the industry it has created is costly; it can nonetheless generate disappointment and false hope, because finding that ultimate *treasure* may be quite elusive.

Real freedom is ultimately and undeniably found within – within the heart and soul. Nobody can give it or sell it, nor can anyone *take* it. It's not for sale.

I believe there are mentors, friends, psychics, therapists, family members and spiritual teachers who can impart and share seeds of wisdom, while pointing the way to seek *that, which is real.* Though, to be trapped in another alluring addiction or dogma is of no value. Remaining open to everything and caught in nothing, will surely inspire an open heart and not a follower of false hope.

The mortal and spiritual teacher or priest, who points the way to God, may often be idolized like a guru – and some spiritual leaders certainly exploit this trust. On the other hand I heard one spiritual teacher purposefully ask people to look where he is pointing, instead of choosing to worship his pointing hand. I wonder who heard those words of genuine guidance.

While on one of my trips to India, I was greatly moved by the story of a humble man from Denmark. Alfred Sorensen moved to England at an early age and worked for twenty years as a down-to-earth gardener in Dartington - a beautiful scenic Southern part of England. It was there that he met and was deeply stirred by the gifted Indian poet, Rabindranath Tagore. After that moment of inspiration during the 1930's, Sorensen left his home in England, after which he spent most of his life in India. He met the Sage Ramana Maharshi in Arunachala. Sorenson found inner and lasting peace through this meeting.

Living in absolute simplicity as he traveled to different parts of this vast land, Sorenson's silence and his inner tranquility radiated from his soul and ultimately attracted various students of mysticism. He was seen as a true Sadhu in India - a man of spiritual wisdom with an unpretentious presence. Sorensen, whose name became Shunyata while in India, consistently said: *"I have nothing to teach and nothing to sell"*.

A purity of expression and his deep-seated fulfillment attracted a small group of Americans in the 1980s who were themselves traveling through India and clearly recognized Shunyata's shining spirit. They eagerly brought him to their home in America, transplanting him in their native California. They evidently and sincerely felt that his presence would be a benefit to many in their own land.

With no concept of highways or even contemporary vehicles, while attempting to walk across a busy road he was hit by a fast car and died in California soon after his arrival. Walking everywhere on foot, he was accustomed to a slower pace. Shunyata was in his nineties when he died. I can't help but feel that he came to America to bring a drop of silence and grace into a hectic and noisy environment.

Freedom already exists within the flow of life; what we so ardently search for is already *in* our deepest being, waiting to be re-discovered. This humble and extraordinary revelation illuminates my own path of awareness.

Modern media successfully utilizes the human and potent desire for freedom, as a sales pitch. Cars, food and holidays are depicted with a focus on emancipation. Who could resist that look of carefree pleasure shamelessly displayed in the face of someone riding their horse, hair flying in the wind while stepping through dwindling breakers on the sandy shoreline – advertising a vacation to purchase. Or a sports car climbing the hills of Southern France with eye-catching exhilaration displayed on the driver's face – advertising a car for sale. This surely represents the epitome of freedom to a public who lusts after even more worldly goods.

By making use of the longing for liberty, the creators of adverts have figured out clever techniques to market their product. Being fully aware of man's desire for peace and freedom - a promise of fulfillment is waved around like a colorful flag.

Somewhere in the depths of our collective and existing wisdom there is the knowledge that to be really free is not to be tricked by a mirage or even imagine there is something illusory to attain. Being at peace with the moment itself is to have found serenity - here and now.

Freedom can't be bought no matter how much money is spent in the process. A beautiful tree has no need to sell its blossom or fruit. A blossom-laden tree, 'attempting to sell tickets' to anyone wishing to inhale the fragrant flowers or gaze at the beautiful colors it emits, would be laughable. The fragrance and vision of a tree in blossom is available to *all* who can see and recognize it. So is freedom! Having said all that, I am still trying to find it myself, and am reminded of Voltaire who said: *"You can search the world over for that diamond, only to find it in your own back garden"*'.

'*No* –thing to teach, and *no*-thing to sell'

"In order to find yourself,
get lost in the forest of life"
Mike Dolan

Veterans of War

Watching the various documentaries in memory of VJ and VE day in 1994 was a humbling experience, and people were stirred by the courage of a generation, now classified as senior citizens.

People felt moved by the fifty-year commemoration of a harsh struggle for peace and freedom. During numerous interviews conducted by television networks, these now elderly soldiers spoke with gravity, with sincerity and without bitterness about a war they fought fifty years ago. Veterans who had fought the War in Europe and in Asia were receiving the tribute and respect they so deserved.

Viewers were dismayed at the unmerciful conditions the old veterans had been forced to cope with and what they had suffered in prison camps as young men. The sheer adversity these warriors so bravely endured, may not even be imaginable.

Footage of these actual events, including those of Burma, further intensified my interest of a momentous episode in the history of man. *Real* people had been involved and now fifty years later they were looking back, and speaking without self-pity, about those brutal circumstances.

These men and women had memories that would never leave them, could never leave them and yet they managed to live 'ordinary lives' as best they could, and had done so for the last fifty years.

Tears filled my eyes at the sight of shining, age-worn faces alight with the knowledge of their endurance. As they marched gallantly through the streets of London I saw noble and dignified features without a trace of arrogance; men and women in their seventies and eighties commemorating a victory – their victory. They had much to be proud of, I thought. Some of the old warriors died during this event as the heat was intense that summer.

Many of us were filled with gratitude for the living example of strength and fortitude that they so willingly gave to their Nation and even more poignant, a legacy to the generation who had yet to born.

I saw the glistening of a tear in the furrowed and valiant faces as they marched by. Clearly they had team-mates involved in this historic and bloody event, friends who had not come home. I believe it was for them and in their honor too that these soldiers were now marching and paying their respects.

"WHEN YOU GO HOME
TELL THEM OF US, AND SAY FOR YOUR TOMORROW,
WE GAVE OUR TODAY"

They fought bravely to give this country autonomy. I can't help but wince when I see a self-important greed displayed by the very children who inherited this legacy, a gift that was acquired through great hardship by their grandparents. Perhaps these 'children' may not truly understand the value of this contribution, or the sacrifice it involved.

On that very same day as the parades were in full swing, newspapers were packed with reports of scandals, fraud and exploitation of the welfare system. Some unscrupulous people were living luxuriously on the result of this cheating.

The welfare system began after World War Two and was born of compassion. These very people now in their seventies and eighties had fought the War, and had also spent their whole lives paying into their country and an organization that was intended to take care of the needs of the truly disadvantaged. It was a caring attempt to correct a class system that had badly neglected those who were impoverished. A working health care system, the NHS that evolved after World War Two, was a generous gift from a whole generation.

Sadly, people had come flocking into Britain to receive gratis dental work during the 1960's and even 1970's when dental care was 'free of charge' (supposedly for those who paid into the NHS system). In fact it was free of charge for anyone and everyone. It was exploited.

A young Swiss boy, who had come to learn English at an expensive school for foreign and affluent students, gloated over his elaborate and expensive dental work in Britain - at no cost to him. He thought the English were rather stupid and was certainly going to take advantage. Having wealthy parents in Switzerland, he was not disadvantaged nor was he entitled to free dental care in Britain; nobody was refused at that time. Health care was given unreservedly, trustingly and with compassion. Soon there were flights coming into Britain with pregnant women, who knew they would receive free delivery of their babies. After which, they boarded flights back to their own country.

Was the foundation of this system a little naïve? During the mid-1990s I remember hearing pregnant young teenagers talking roughly in the streets of England, while complaining that the government wanted to cut down on welfare favors. I believe they had no idea that someone had worked hard to pay for those benefits.

The British welfare system generously provided adequate housing and financial support to those in need; a resource that was severely abused by later generations. It quickly became an accepted custom or culture to leave school at an early age and sign up on the welfare system. I shuddered at the stories about boyfriends being supported by some welfare mums. Boyfriends who lay around drunk and jobless, producing more innocent and vulnerable babies. Babies were the blameless members of this caper. I was distressed to see some young mothers treating their children as assets in order to receive housing.

The original scheme of the benefit system was to help young mothers who had lost a husband in the War; the system had become overburdened with a new generation -seeing it as a way of life. The newspapers were packed with reports of people from other countries rushing into Britain - *'England offered abundant benefits'* was the rampant talk and incentive. Sadly, many saw this as an easy market for scams. Somebody had to pay for it.

The misuse of something initiated from compassion, is disappointing. Money poured into a benefit system over fifty years could have been focused more wisely, for those who were now in need of it and indeed had paid for it - Veterans of the Second World War. They certainly deserve care and consideration as their bodies become frail. We owe it to them, not as a grudging obligation but a heartfelt act of love and appreciation for what they gave willingly - so many years ago.

Watching the parade, I felt proud of humanity. When reading the newspapers – who wouldn't feel a little ashamed of humanity? The human make-up is a tapestry of attributes and it's certainly a choice, which aspects to embrace and which to strengthen.

WHEN YOU GO HOME,
TELL THEM OF US AND SAY FOR YOUR TOMORROW,
WE GAVE OUR TODAY"

Clothes at the Beach

The beach was fairly empty that day as a sprightly middle-aged couple, covered from the neck to their feet in stylishly bright colored striped towel robes, calmly and methodically began changing into swimming gear. The only body parts exposed were their head, neck and feet.

After working deftly inside this purposely-designed outfit, they finally emerged in chic bathing suits.

Though it seemed comical at the time, especially seen from the perspective of my American companion, this very enactment of decorum was so very English and yet a little absurd. Actually it was probably quite sensible.

Memories of childhood days during the 1960s', on the beautiful Dorset Coast of Lyme Regis came flooding back to me. How very ordinary it was at that time to see crowds on a beach discovering countless ways to conceal their bodies, while absorbed in the elaborate process of changing into swimsuits.

Now, thirty years later this outdated *modus operandi* being performed so meticulously on this pebbly beach in

Budleigh Salterton seemed quaint; particularly baffling though was the fact that the beach was almost empty. A resolute effort to avoid exposing any part of the human body while changing clothes on the beach, though graciously accomplished, seemed a bit pointless in the 21st century where beaches are inundated with nubile bodies covered by mere *fig leaves*. Not much is left to the imagination as swimwear is designed to be enticingly alluring.

This dignified display on the beach and the custom itself, was possibly redundant.

Just
For The Fun of It!

I first met my mother's well-read and sophisticated friend in 1992; a lady who was not only highly motivated and curious, she also craved innovative knowledge. Her keen awareness of alternative medicine astounded and impressed me since I also have an affinity for mankind's symbiotic relationship with nature's remedies.

Jane was absorbed in the research of a recently publicized therapy called *Aura Soma* - a combination of color and remedial fragrant oils in a bottle. While discussing creative blends of aromatic oils, Jane mentioned her plans to write a book on the subject and encouraged me at the same time, to create my own unique mix of colors and healing fragrances. After eagerly producing samples of colorfully sweet-smelling oils, we were both thrilled with the outcome.

An observant curiosity coupled with her deep respect and fascination for knowledge had a big impact on me. Being in Jane's company was enlivening for anyone who had the good fortune to know her. With a bright clear intellect, she was always willing to see beyond the normal structures of our conditioned mindset; she must have been approaching eighty-four years old and was manifestly receptive to life's mysteries.

While maintaining our contact in the years ahead, we corresponded throughout my trips to India. Her continuous and exuberant interest in my travels and growing knowledge of herbal medicine, gave me so much encouragement. I am grateful to this day this wonderful lady's effort in writing letters to me while I was in India for a whole year. I didn't receive any form of communication, let alone letters, from my own parents. It was a comfort to know that someone cared.

Jane longed to know more about computers so that she could write a travelogue of her own adventures in Asia and in particular one enthralling and dangerous journey through Afghanistan during the 1940's. I was fascinated by *her* travels and we were both excited when our articles featured in the local magazine 'The Estuary'.

I had purchased my first computer in 1991, which proved to be an instant catalyst, so I offered to write some of her narratives. Jane seemed very interested in buying a word processor for herself; we both felt this would be a wonderful way to make her life even more motivating. A few days later she decided against this endeavor.

Jane said: *"I can't buy something just for the fun of it"*. This didn't sound like my inimitable friend!

Is it amiss to be impulsively and joyfully unrestrained at the age of eighty-four? After encountering her spirit of adventure, I was surprised that Jane couldn't endorse an extravagant purchase for herself, 'for *the fun of it*'!

In spite of a pioneering mind and monetary autonomy, there remained a clearly imprinted mark of frugality and a need to be sensible. Did a well-meaning and levelheaded daughter wish to prevent her mother from being impractical with 'frivolous' acquisitions?

Is there room for pure, innocent and down-to-earth fun in a sagacious world?

The Children

"Children are the living messages
we send to a time
we will not see".

Neil Postman

A wholesome innocence in children and elderly people seemed to prompt my empathy at that time. Seeing these members of society as pure and uncorrupted – I realized that my outlook was somewhat idealistic and I've had plenty of opportunities to experience a more realistic perspective since then. Nevertheless, there is often a genuine quality of spontaneity more natural to children and even some elderly people than other age groups, which endears me to them.

On numerous and short trips to Topsham I visited my sister and mother, who were taking care of children at the time. The interesting characters I encountered with these emergent and growing human beings was deeply touching.

Thinly built and tense Philip, found it difficult to be spontaneous and tried to engage attention by running across the room while peering in our direction to see if anyone noticed him. At only three years, an overt need of approval seemed important in his young life. Could he be an aspiring and timid performer? I know that some well-known actors have indeed stated in interviews that they excel on stage, yet avoid public encounters at other times. Philip needed applause, and yet shied away from authentic, sincere recognition. He was a sensitive and intelligent boy for sure.

Three-year-old Ben, fondly nicknamed *big Ben* (because there was also a *little Ben* in the group) was relaxed and laughed instinctively. He danced with delight and without any need for overt recognition. Cavorting around the room and totally absorbed in his innovative and happy world, Ben clearly felt free to express his inner sparkle. Where Philip sought endorsement from the adult environment, Ben seemed secure and happy in his individuality.

Mum would sing lovely songs in her lilting harmonious voice as the children jumped up and down in delight, singing along with her.

Jennifer and Tamara, the two daughters of a local doctor and attorney, were full of life and cheer. Tamara ran to hug those people she recognized and with a welcoming smile she asked abundant and competent questions; she had an inventive and enquiring spirit. Jennifer was usually skipping around and beaming with gentle sunny smiles that brought a bright ray of sunshine into the world. I'm sure she continues to warm people's hearts' as she grows older. Jennifer was caring and motherly, tenderly looking after the younger ones. My sister had taken care of Jennifer and Tamara since their birth, and there were surely more experiences than just sunny smiles and exuberant hugs, but for me those heartfelt and intelligent little children, now bring forth a wave of fond memories that will always be treasured.

Sporty Joe, nicknamed *JoeJoe* was enthusiastic about athletics - he was the sportsman! With a courageous mind, a robust body and active fervor he would somersault across the room and practice his sporty techniques. There was a special place in my heart for Joe. I understood and admired the plucky nature he demonstrated so early in his young life. Such a fearless spirit will make an inspiring impact on others throughout his life. He was *being himself* while instinctively saying whatever he felt. A striking and shining bright star.

Joe had an older sister called Katie - a shy and delicate little girl, even aloof at times. She needed her space to reflect on things. With a sensitive disposition, she observed everything with large bright eyes and although she didn't dive into boisterous activities with the other children, she was most certainly a character in her own right. Flowers enchanted Katie as she walked around the garden delighting in their colors and fragrances. Katie and Joe had young, happy parents who owned a local hotel in Topsham. I often saw the family enjoying village events. These two creative children had a wonderful start in life.

Stephen called my sister 'mummy' - Maggie had an especially soft spot for him. He was dropped off at seven thirty in the morning and picked up at seven thirty in the evening; it was a long day every day. Stephen's hardworking Mum had a demanding full time job and my sister realized that this little boy needed some motherly nurturing.

Sophie, another child who touched my heart, began life with some health problems. Today Sophie is a beautiful, healthy and well-balanced teenager. I befriended Sophie's parents during that time and we are close friends to this day.

When my sister went on a two-week holiday to Greece, the parents entrusted me to take care of three little children. We had a lovely time - off to the park while they played on slides and swings, then to a local café for teas. We all enjoyed ourselves and I missed them very much when those two weeks came to an end. During that time I chatted merrily with the parents when they came to collect their offspring.

Year after year I would return for brief visits to Topsham and see the children growing older; each with their own unique personality.

Child minders are extraordinary people who nurture children while their Mum works during the day. Personally I would have found it difficult not to develop attachments or not to feel really sad when they reached school age, ready for the next stage of their journey into adulthood.

It's clear that children come into the world already equipped with individual personalities – after which their environment shapes them, further.

"I brought children into this dark world
because it needed the light
that only a child can bring".

Liz Armbruster

Victoria's Medicinal Garden

Victoria and her husband were taking the first step to accomplishing their longed for vision. Establishing a flourishing and productive garden and cultivating organically grown medicinal herbs had been their shared dream for a long time.

After purchasing a piece of land in South Devon, clearly a place of tranquility for humans and plants, they invested a substantial sum of money in shrubs, seeds and the basic components needed to develop this project. Traveling all the way to Scotland to procure quality plants from a highly recommended grower, they purchased some rare and expensive medicinal herbs. It was not only money that was lovingly entrusted to this calling but their skill, courage and above all their hearts. Yes they were meticulous and had no intention of buying from sources other than those offering the highest standard, which is why they spent so much of their time, initially, in research.

The herbs grew remarkably well. Rare and often difficult to cultivate flora began to grow into robust and hearty specimens – evidently a response to something more than just green fingers. The garden developed and prospered until the ghastly ordeal began.

Three years after their arrival, a neighbor in her late sixties who owned the property next door, launched a crusade that was to last a further eight exhausting years for Victoria and her husband. It was a campaign to systematically destroy all the herbs that had thus far been growing in the garden. One of her methods was to pour strong poisonous weed killer into an organically prepared compost mound that had been carefully set up. The neighbor, a practicing and religious Baptist wanted to seize the land for herself so she could extend her own property. There seemed an explicit intent to destroy the couple along with their inspirational foresight.

A desire to facilitate the healing of sickness and disease would surely be an act of generous compassion? To establish and cultivate their own property for this vision was a project of love. The munificence of these two people in their longing to share land, knowledge and hard work for the good of others – was striking.

The hardhearted neighbor nearing her seventieth year of life, chose to deride the very purpose of this medicinal garden; an embittered woman finding an exploitable target for merciless actions. She called Victoria a witch.

Are we still living in the furtive shadows of Medieval England where corrupt and unscrupulous men of power misused this very authority, employing it instead to force crooked ideas onto a fearful and timid public? A dark era where dominance and wealth gave sanction to cruelty. Are there still illicit witch-hunts and scornful talk about people who try to work with nature? The Christian sentiment of *love thy neighbor* seemed to be missing in the heart and vocabulary of this devoutly practicing Baptist neighbor. Though greed, avarice and vengeance are not Christian attributes – this outwardly religious lady with conspicuous double standards, owned many more choice properties in the area. On nearing one's seventieth year, would one not begin to ponder on certain aspects of life itself? Actually I would hope that at any time in my own life, the wish to impart kindness rather than avariciousness would be predominant. There are manifold men and women who share this sentiment, yet the attributes of greed and perhaps even fear, emerge as hidden aspirations of a lifetime – for some.

It was with enormous joy that Victoria spoke and I listened to the miracle of therapeutic herbs – as though they were her children. We both knew the precious and restorative qualities of the flourishing Ginseng in her garden. I saw her marvelous Gingko tree, Golden Seal and many other beneficial plants that were alive and abounding. Being an herbalist myself I was delighted to have found Victoria and share the same love for a sacred gift of nature.

I contacted numerous and ethical organic herbal growers in California while living there in the 1980s', but when I spoke to Victoria and her husband, and indeed met them, I knew that there was something unique about their garden. They worked with the purest love – as some people really do.

When I went to see Victoria for the last time, I saw a broken, tear filled woman who couldn't understand why one human being would have summoned such persecution or even maintain this kind of assault.

Victoria represented the true Christian sentiment of caring. When encountering this predicament, I felt compelled to question whether the notion of being a Christian has been horribly corrupted over the last two thousand years. It was ultimately as a down to earth and practicing herbalist myself, that I did wonder at the medieval attitude still existing in Britain, whereas Switzerland as a country always has, and still does offer herbal teas and supplements in almost every pharmacy. The Swiss traditionally grow up with medicinal herbs; I know because I lived there for seventeen years.

Things have changed in England now that numerous natural health clinics have opened in the last decade, and MDs' are exploring the avenue of preventative health care. Fortunately there is much more receptivity surrounding the knowledge of herbs in Britain now.

Victoria's herb garden was possibly twenty years too early.

"The Earth has enough for mankind's need,
but not for mankind's greed"

Mahatma Gandhi

Crop Protection

Opening a magazine and faced with the captivating picture of a country scene gleaming with uncontaminated and natural purity, I saw a vibrantly lush picture of meadows, rivers and trees.

Boldly outlined at the top of the picture were the heartening words *'Crop Protection'* - evoking a heartfelt sense of enrichment and safety for the intrinsically rustic quality of the land. Wheat and oat fields ripening in the sun's warmth, farmers working hard and content with their harvest presented a picture of sanguine harmony. I could well imagine that organizations such as *'Friends of the Earth'* or *Greenpeace'*

73

were communicating a healthy message to the public forum with this announcement because there was a distinct focus on the preservation of our beautiful planet. Surfing on a wave of sentimental nostalgia, I recognized the English countryside I loved and knew so well.

In stark reality this advertisement was meant to be an innovative tactic to promote chemical fertilizers and harsh pest control. A disappointing announcement that appeared initially to voice the spirit of organic 'green and clean' was in actuality, only making use of it for conflicting and self-serving motives. Shocked at this discovery, I was yet again, reminded of human nature in all its ambiguous obscurity. I burst out with incredulous laughter at the sheer audacity of this obvious paradox.

The latest and most trendy marketing gimmick is a mockery and clearly a crafty guise to gain public support. After all to be 'green minded' and free of pesticides is becoming popular. Capitalizing on green issues in order to promote the unequivocal contradiction, must demonstrate the epitome of public deception and an assumption that this thinly veiled guise will not be exposed. Do advertisers believe that people are so brainless as to not see though such ploys?

This blatant strategy of advertising chemical fertilizers and pesticides as something environmentally friendly, surely reveals the 'con artist' in an alarmingly substantial position. Is this really a new market to be readily utilized for commercial goals and is the general public really so easily manipulated...I think not ......hope not!

The Hopeful 'Guru'

An unconventional Eastern Indian man in his late fifties launched a small publishing company based in the north of England. Optimistic authors were welcomed and encouraged to visit this friendly publisher where his hospitable girlfriend as well as his son created a warm environment for writers to gather and read elements of their books out loud. A heartening lure to those of us who were hopeful new authors - indeed we were all aspiring authors.

The man saw himself as author, publisher *and* living sage. Admittedly, some things he said made sense on a metaphysical level, and he certainly had some wise words in his repertoire. Behaving somewhat as an unrivalled seer, his spiritual assertions coupled with an air of self-importance made his listeners uneasy. We were obligated to sit silently in a friendly circle while he spoke. The authors, though courteous, were primarily optimistic in their hope that this visit may clinch a publishing arrangement and launch their book.

Consciously or unconsciously, he used his position as a publisher to entice eager writers who were just starting out;

listening to his imperious evening lecture was a requisite. I was simply wishing to be acknowledged and accepted in the publishing milieu, without requiring a spiritual guru.

Relinquishing candor for the manifestation of a craving can be a snare. I believe that this incident pointed out the human sentiment of *desire*, an emotion that can entrap those who are willing to market their integrity.

The publisher's own son, a gentle intelligent boy of twenty-three, and his girlfriend, both bestowed the desired reverence. They saw in this man, a world teacher. Or were they submissively acquiescing to a narcissistic man?

Initially, the yearning to be published clouded my willingness to speak out; his desire to be a Guru and certainly his shrewd means to gratify this objective was a precarious deception. Gullible new authors were momentarily being caught in this net - his net. A mutual trap, each attempting to fulfill their own personal craving

He felt slighted by my frank and straightforward opinion once my composure dissolved. A playful yet sincere tendency to 'burst a bubble' and expose truth when confronted by a scam, is irresistible to me. In this case I was faced with someone who elevates their own person while patronizing that of others.

This man may not have intentionally set out to deceive anyone; it may have been an illusory way to gain attention and even praise. To my knowledge, he never did publish anyone's book - except his own.

Oh No,
Not that Again!

Do we call it love…? Romance…..Sensuality? I've even heard the well-worn terms 'soul mates' or 'my twin flame' used over and over again. Can we even put a name to that feeling of light-filled joy or the unplanned disconsolate sensation of pain and loss when it tears apart?

After hearing numerous personal portrayals recounting the drama and heartache of unrequited love, it's evident that we all recognize the rare and familiar feeling of romantic affection, where your heart bursts into blossom like a flower. Light pours into your soul, there is a skip in your step and hips swing lyrically as though dancing along with poetic music while performing even mundane tasks. The color of your eyes become a beautiful shade lighter, sparkling with a magical glow. Adorning your body with attractive clothes becomes a blissful venture and energy levels mysteriously transform into heightened vitality. It must be close to paradise. The warmth of a smile shines in the heart and faces of those who are *in-love*. This is the state of being smitten and love-struck!

Then the *fall*. Oh yes, that again. How many times have I heard and seen the agonizing cry of someone who declared how genuine it all was – 'it felt real'. Unrelenting and sudden thoughts of doubt tiptoe through your mind – *'was it all an illusion or was it just a temporary state of bliss'?*

Disbelief and a longing for paradise lost run rampant, without any hope of fulfillment. Questions persist, *'how did it go wrong'?* A determined heavy weight and a gloomy dark cloud afflicts that dancing heart; each hour, each minute is a fresh reminder. There is nowhere to hide. Waves of sadness are impossible to ignore.

Time itself offers the only hope of healing, and finally after exhausting all possible emotions the release and relief of *letting go* brings comfort to the destitute heart. Peace finally wraps its soft arms around you, as does wisdom and new hope. Soothing solace of music finds its way into your heart again.

Songs that relate to your pain suddenly come into audible range. A new and different emotion of guarded trepidation eventually emerges. Who would wish for that pain again! A sense of maturity and caution appears - until the next time!

The revelation transpires that you are not alone. Our collective and tough human journey is to feel the ecstasy and agony of love in all its glory. It happens again and again and again because this is our human predicament as the soul emerges into realization beyond emotion. Is love for 'another' really the mirror and fiery awakening of the seed that grows into the flowering of love in its purest and egoless state?

Passion has and will always emanate from my own heart and soul, yet now I find myself preferring the passion and love of dance, nature, flowers, trees, writing, humanity, photography and the understanding of life itself.........am I being cowardly in my desire to rise above the wild waters of reckless passion that is directed towards another person? Having been in the throes of immature love, I now believe there is a higher love than the neediness or grasping to satisfy desires of sensuality, and that 'higher love' is what I reach for.

Love in its depth of consciousness will never stop seeking recognition. It is the path of ultimate awareness.

"Take the breath of the new dawn

and make it part of you

it will give you strength"

From HOPI words of Wisdom

The Grand Hotel

     Watching the rhythmic movement of tides flowing in and out while seated on a big soft chair at the Grand Hotel in a popular South Devon resort, I enjoyed an ample pot of hot tea. Through the large bay window the brisk bathers could be seen frolicking and racing into the cold English ocean during summer months.

It was one of those wonderful hotels offering plenty of available and individual alcoves. Even as rain drizzled outside, the view imparted a comforting ambiance of gray softness with the added cheer of a bright glowing fire inside. What a haven it was. Surrounded by the daily hustle and bustle of our progressive world, I found myself resting in this sanctuary for a couple of hours.

On one of those occasions a brown tanned lady sat nearby; with timeworn wrinkles etched in the record of her physical form, she glowed with youthful charm. In a moment of curiosity, I spoke to this bright and vibrant lady. With the well-worn habit of Englishness I commented on the weather. There began an intriguing rapport between the two of us where I learnt about the fascinating life she had lead. With a soft husky voice, Eva related how she had spent years in South America, Africa and India, walking up and down beaches in Goa, climbing up into the hills of Kulu Manali and being stranded while exploring a mountain in South America. She recalled her travels with passion. An avid photographer too, who clearly expressed more than a mere picture. I loved gazing at those living memories as her animated photos accompanied lively descriptions of hiking expeditions. she spoke with clarity and delight.

I'll always remember the photo she showed me on one particular afternoon, which was accompanied by a wave of merry laughter. A picture taken two years earlier in Southern India personified a sun-tanned woman with a bright red swimsuit draped over her leanly built and shrunken body. A body that nevertheless emanated strength and spirit! Who would not marvel at the vitality conveyed by this seventy-nine year old lady who could laugh so heartily at herself in that oversized red bathing suit?

She had earnestly begun art classes in the town she now lived in - Torquay; I believe that her next project was to paint pictures using images from all her favorite photos.

I felt a little sad when my two-hour break came to an end and I was duty-bound to return to someone who seemed lacking in contentment, in spite of a trouble-free lifetime of prosperity and ease. I was working as a caregiver at the time.

What a contrast between these two elderly ladies.

"Your face is masked with lines of life,
put there by love and laughter; suffering and tears.
It's beautiful"

Lynsay Sands

The Package Tour

With an added interest in the rich history of Turkey, we anticipated two weeks of sunshine, especially after the travel agent assured us of a room at a charming guesthouse in the hills of Turunc Bay.

On landing at Dalaman Airport, the group was met with dazzling smiles of our English tour representatives, Peter and Trish. Their smiles certainly matched the bright sunny weather and we were won over by a seemingly friendly overture. Breathing a sigh of relief and the cheery thought of a restful venture', I recalled the years of traveling backpack and budget style, where consistent alertness was essential and daily preparations were often required. Being spared those hurdles seemed a luxury.

Chatting throughout the trip, our tour guides accompanied the mixed collection of twenty tourists on a two-hour mini-bus ride from the airport. Offering useful tips and information while answering questions, they heartily entertained the group. Having been social workers in Britain they now decided to work in the travel industry during summer months. What a good idea I thought.

Enthralled gasps from the visitors in the minivan were aroused as the rugged scenery surrounded and loomed in front of us. Enraptured by spectacular views, we all peered through dusty windows while circling the ever steeper hills, until our final descent into a stunning cove. Trish pointed to the charming guesthouse perched aesthetically in the hills of Turunc Bay, which was to be our dwelling for two weeks.

Once our lodging had been allocated, it mysteriously turned into a cramped studio instead of a one-bedroom suite. Our private veranda inexplicably became the public pathway to the dining room. Seemingly uninterested in their guests, Trish and Peter swiftly went missing - only appearing sporadically. Their hasty lack of allegiance to the guests in contrast to an overt show of loyalty towards the guesthouse owner, was lamentably transparent. Was it a policy to ignore guests once they reached their destination? We *were* trapped after all.

During the two-week sojourn we spotted Peter and Trish sunbathing on a secluded beach nearby - or were they hiding? Finally tracking them down and voicing a pitiable disappointment, Ahmed the owner, (equipped with a flamboyant smile), offered us an upgrade at a rather high fee. I began to grasp the reality of the package tour industry.

With a repertoire of suitable and pre-set responses, Trish in a bored attempt to rally us into obedient acquiescence, utilized some skilled terminology, which was a mixture of newly learnt verbiage as tour operators mingled with the language of a social worker. Unbeknownst to them, we weren't prone to resigning ourselves to an unscrupulous situation.

I was alarmed at the vision of trusting vacationers working hard all year, finally embarking on a long awaited package tour and then being left to fend for themselves while unsuspecting that their interests may not be the prime or even secondary concern of the organizers.

Though at the mercy of Trish and Peter, our fellow travelers may have been too worn-out to challenge any discrepancy, or perhaps they didn't mind. They were absorbed in the sunny scenery – for now. When taken for granted by indifferent tour operators, these good-natured visitors will often make do with discomfort in order to oblige. I thought they deserved better.

In spite of the glitch, we enjoyed our high-spirited holiday. Visiting the nearby village and chatting with local people, many of whom spoke German as well as their native Turkish, enriched our interest in the history of this ancient country. Tasty food in the nearby restaurants was worth savoring and of course there was an abundance of delicious Turkish delight. Swimming in the clear fresh waters of the ocean, acquiring a rich brown tan, making friends with the local people and exploring the beautiful rocky terrain, gave us two weeks of recreation. Though we did stay away from our guest house and the phony tour operators. Having caused a ripple in this otherwise smoothly running show, we were now fully aware of the prime interest and I wasn't willing to conceal my discovery.

A pre-conceived idea that social workers addressed fellow human beings in a particularly sensitive way was proved amiss. Trish and Peter indicated this quality to be a mere veneer and once the surface was scratched, some less likable traits were readily revealed. Perhaps they had been the recipients of harsh treatment themselves in the past, and were carrying the effects of it – or had they simply learnt a script to deal with 'demanding' tourists?

The Package tour with all its seeming advantages may not turn out to be so rewarding. Backpack travel affords the priceless opportunity of encountering diverse cultures while embracing an all-encompassing experience. Senses become alert whilst meeting the full spectrum of danger, sincerity, warmth and kindness. One discovers inner qualities of strength, courage and determination. I'm not sure that the package tour allows for that innate experience.

Guns

The British seemed concerned about increasing gun crime in England. A fearful apprehension of an American style *gun happy* nation was being splashed all over British newspapers. Mostly there was a mounting unease regarding recent and easy access to guns and the necessity for British law enforcement to carry weapons themselves.

Growing up as a teenager in the 1960s, I thought guns were for cowboys or else the corrupt and law breaking streets of America; certainly not for polite British society.

While riding the Swiss tram in 1993, several benign looking young men with a rifle perched on their laps, were looking thoughtfully out of the window. Each and every member of the Swiss youth were obligated to practice target shooting in their role as a member of the national and compulsory armed forces. The rifle, normally seen as a hostile device, was in *this* scenario more like a harmless bag of shopping. The young men were on their way to target practice.

Having moved to Zurich, Switzerland at eighteen years old, I grew accustomed to seeing young men on their way to routine target practice at weekends. At that time all men had their military guns and ammunition stored in an underground cellar below their place of residence. It was necessary for every Swiss man to be equipped and prepared for a possible call to war. The Swiss nation was justifiably proud to have a full army at the ready within twenty-four hours; it had been their deliverance in World War Two.

In all my seventeen years in Zurich I never did see anyone misuse or abuse his ownership of a gun. Even in 1993, there seemed no sign of violence or furtiveness in those young men's faces; it was just another dutiful and perhaps boring day of target practice. It was the custom and of course their responsibility to complete this military and mandatory requirement.

Scott, my husband at that time, had been on active duty in the US Navy for a number of years and had only just arrived in Switzerland with me. He was taken aback while riding in the tram when he saw guns resting placidly on young men's laps. I could feel his body tense up as though anxious and on guard. Other passengers were obviously unperturbed. After a few weeks of life in Zurich, Scott recognized the marked cultural contrast of the Swiss mentality to his experience in America, and he relaxed into a new understanding of a different society than his own.

I wonder how safe this practice is nowadays. I know that England as a nation has become provoked into the unlawful and lawful use of guns. Now with open border in Europe, Switzerland too will be alerted to necessary and more current procedures.

Martha Gellhorn

A journalist, novelist and one of the Great War correspondents of our time, Martha Gellhorn captured the attention of many by her unique expression. Honesty was a trait that reflected in her writing.

I saw her in 1995 on a television program called *'Face to Face'*, an unassuming yet profound talk show where extraordinary people were quietly interviewed. Martha Gellhorn at eighty-seven years old, shone with a potent presence and spoke in a clear resonant voice. Her responses were refreshingly succinct. Vibrantly clear vision gave me a distinct impression that she could communicate quite plainly with those reflective dark eyes. Actually she was ageless. Yes, one of those rare people who glow with dynamic realization and emanate a spirit that is timeless – as the spirit truly is endless and eternal.

During her early years she 'turned up' in a war zone because she felt the media reporting at that time was not satisfactory nor was it trustworthy. She wanted to know what was really going on in those hazardous conditions and as she herself related, an insatiable curiosity had *'eaten her all her life'*. It was not courage that inspired these actions – she explained that her burning incentive was inquisitiveness and her motives were not to impress anyone or grab at fame or money, as she was driven by a fervent curiosity.

After working in Paris for a number of different magazines, she had been fired from most of them for being a bad writer. Perhaps she hadn't been willing to forfeit her truth for the sake of writing whatever seemed popular at the time. Candor isn't always a welcome trait in any era.

My admiration for this woman was immense. Though confronting great hardship, poverty and rejection she hadn't sold her soul in order to gain status, yet she ultimately achieved a highly respected place in the world without forfeiting her ardent spirit. Martha Gellhorn's presence that evening was an inspiration; heartened by her words I felt authenticated with some personal thoughts in my own life at that time.

Over the centuries, the harsh challenges of adversity confronted by artists have tested their dedication to the very limits of human endurance. Vincent Van Gogh was a tortured soul who lived on meager takings; a human being who gave his life to art and who will go down in history as a living testimonial. Contemporary owners of his paintings may now take great pride in describing 'the masterpiece', while contemplatively glancing at their accoutrement. Proud owners of renowned pieces of artwork often relate the troubled story of impassioned artists – yet an indication of authentic empathy may be sadly lacking and for some, it's just another material investment.

A few days later and on the very same talk show, I was profoundly moved by the appearance of another spirited and elderly person - Alicia Markova. A distinguished ballet dancer and now an eighty-six year old woman, Markova's soft glowing face, sparkling eyes and musical voice was enthralling. Once more, deeply stirred by someone who had lived a life of impassioned commitment while risking the loss of material comfort, I was enthused with admiration. At eighty-six years old, a vibrant soul shone through her eyes and a life of delighted commitment was visibly potent in her face. Seeing two women who tangibly maintained that very essence of life, that fire and passion within their soul - I felt quietly acknowledged in my aspirations.

Alicia Markova explained that when her mentor died, the ballet company collapsed while leaving her penniless and very young. She recalled dancing in cinemas for very little money and whatever she did earn was spent on ballet shoes. She told her story with quiet radiance.

Two remarkable people who in their late eighties, emanated graciousness, beauty and above all fulfillment.

I believe that Princess Diana was one of those rare and courageous people, living life with irreplaceable authenticity and by doing so, risking social displeasure. Her warmth was a magnet and always would have been - had she lived.

We humans may easily misconstrue that which is truly authentic in this life. In the end we may even ask ourselves that burning question: *"What is the difference between a temporary buzz and a moment of genuine bliss? What is indeed real?"* Lamentably, importance is often attached to 'fool's gold'.

It may be tempting to spend one's life chasing after a fleeting illusion of gratification and as bodily life wanes, what's left if the soul's longing for vitality has been overlooked?

Some rare people reach those heights of human potential through valor and dedication and thereby touch upon something that is inspirational to others. These remarkable women did just that.

*"Language is originally and essentially
a system of signs or symbols,
which denote real occurrences,
or their echo in the human soul."*

Carl Jung

Dancers

'Dancers' is a Film starring Mikhail Baryshnikov as the lead performer in the storyline and is an extraordinary ballet where willowy nymphs seemed to be blowing across the stage with feather-like grace. Drawn into the charisma of the dance where music and bodies were flowing from one scene to another as a river flows towards the ocean, I was filled with a blissful boost of energy. Jumping through the air with playful passion, Baryshnikov's noble strength pulsated throughout his face and body, a quality often present in Russian male dancers.

It struck me a little later that until ten years before, I could hardly bear seeing a ballet being performed without my aching heart revealing whispers of sadness. Ballet was the love of my life and after age fifteen it became the greatest joy, yet deepest sorrow. A paradox. Watching a performance was an equal ambiguity. If the dancers were heavy or uninspiring, it seemed boring. Yet when performers magically expressed the exquisiteness of dance, it was a raw reminder of what I'd failed to accomplish myself. Certain I'd missed the boat and haunted by regret, I was acutely aware of an ache in my belly, the unvoiced words surfaced: *"I should be there!"*

As maturity and a little more wisdom grew in my consciousness, the understanding became apparent that it wasn't a failure but a poignant misplaced decision to abandon any aspirations as a dancer. Nevertheless, a pining reminder and the sense of loss weighed on my heart for years to follow.

Miss Gibbs, a caring and spirited ballet teacher who encouraged and supported my love of dance, even insisting that I had great talent, went out of her way to arrange an audition with the Sadler's Wells Ballet Company (now the Royal Ballet). It was on that crucial unforgettable day, the day of the audition, that I surrendered to a harsh reality. My mother had just given birth to Dominic, our youngest sibling and not wishing to bother her with the seemingly trivial request of being driven on a three-hour drive to my ballet audition, I was convinced that our mum had more critical things to think about. To give up a love of dance seemed a worthy and noble sacrifice at the time, yet the helplessness of not knowing how to get transport to the audition, alone, contributed to that decision. The fervor to dance was so great, it would consume my life; I imagined that I would have to give it my *all* or step away from it completely.

Several years later, reading about the life of Rudolf Nureyev who had not given up in spite of challenges and adversity, it was clear that the true and devoted strength to pursue this passion was missing in my young heart at age fifteen and so, in that moment the dream of being a dancer was relinquished – or so I thought.

The momentous decision on that day caused a saddening grief until my arrival in Alaska when surprisingly the ache was dispelled. For five exhilarating years I had the good fortune to be faced with the spirit of this icy terrain, night and day - *all* the time. Touching on the peaks and depths as I would have done as a ballet dancer, I found myself immersed and enraptured by nature in its raw form. It was intense, invigorating and very *total!*

To become a truly inspired dancer, I believe that one is pushed to and beyond already known limits. As those unknown expanses of existence are touched, something of the divine is encountered. This is dance! This very opportunity was handed to me by the actual mode of living in such a powerful land as

Alaska. A land of strength where the pure, cold snows of winter lasted for seven lengthy yet enlivening months.

Longing for colors other than white during my first winter, I hankered for a splash of green in the landscape. Oh but I loved those winters where the sun shone for a mere three hours and during that short time, caused the white terrain to sparkle as though reflecting the diamonds of life. With every new winter that followed I could only stand in awe at the sight around me while absorbing this quality of passionate strength. I welcomed this deeper inner vision.

Now as I watched the film 'Dancers', I felt no more separation with those performers who were giving themselves entirely to the dance and to the music - absolute and unreserved in this deliberate and soulful surrender. No ache in my belly anymore; I felt no rift and no need to compare my merits. At last, content.

Today, my love of ballet has hopefully been transformed into a love of life. I try to give this very passion to whatever I do in life, no matter how trivial it may seem.

Reaching the depth of bliss and touching that profound commitment to one's spirit is a place of allegiance that results in the experience of ecstasy. Now, seeing it expressed in others I feel 'at one' with the dance and the dancer.

Heartache is apparent when there is an assumption at having failed and in seeing one's potential accomplishment exhibited by others. When comparing myself to other dancers without having fully lived my own unique experiences in life, there was an empty ache. Now there is pure delight as I see people voice themselves utterly, joyfully and wholly.

Fulfillment is like an ocean – how can there be any separation when we bathe in the same ocean?

"The deeper that sorrow carves into your heart,
the more joy you can contain.
Is not the lute that soothes your spirit,
the very wood that was hollowed with knives? "

Kahlil Gibran
'The Prophet'

"Sweet Little Old Ladies"

"Inside every older person
Is a younger person –
Wondering what the heck happened"

Cora Harvey Armstrong

The enthusiastic idea of working with the elderly would be mutually fulfilling, I thought. I was sure that people became wiser, kinder and even content as the time when a departure from this material world grew a little closer. A natural and even spiritual desire to spend the latter years of worldly existence without regrets or bitterness, seemed meaningful values to a completion of a long life. This impression endeared me to work with older people in whatever capacity opened up. Having also just completed training as a hospice volunteer, I was keen to validate my wholehearted desire to give support to and show compassion in the best way possible.

Recognizing that not all people would value the precious time they had left, I convinced myself that many would, and anticipated spending quality time in a jointly motivating way where conversations, walks and daily errands, would be mutually heartwarming and fun.

While working as a caregiver to well-heeled ladies who were dwelling in their opulent homes - my ideology was quickly shattered with a dose of reality when some 'tyrannical rulers' had me trembling and quivering in disbelief. I was reminded of childhood years at school. Being reduced to a nervous mass of jelly by a despotic female teacher seemed a good comparison.

I recall the unyielding gaze of one castigating eighty-nine-year-old lady whose scolding eyes and rebuking comments were thrust upon her grandson as soon as he walked through the door. A playful glint in his eye and an Irish lilt to his accent, he brought a cheery heartiness into my world that afternoon. His grandmother's comments obviously didn't put a dent in this young man's good-humored temperament. I wish I had been better equipped to dodge such caustic remarks.

Spirited eighty-nine year old ladies resisting the help they required while fighting to maintain control, often resulted in overly dictatorial behavior. Yet I felt a deep admiration for the determined and courageous life they had lived and were now living, to the best of their ability. I felt compassion for the predicament they now found themselves in, and their indomitable dispute with the natural process of ageing. The struggles of getting older can generate irritability and a tendency to be self-absorbed. I also know that strong minded and restless ladies may feel that the weakening of their physical and even mental competence indicates a loss of control. This alarming sense of failure instigates an over stated and determined display of power.

Is it an ironic myth that *sweet little old ladies* are taken advantage of? Well maybe in some cases this can be and is certainly true, but numerous well-heeled ladies unwittingly test the kindheartedness of long-suffering caregivers too.

I've encountered remarkable elderly ladies who express a profound thoughtfulness for others; elderly people who laugh with *joie de vivre* while their clear bright minds bring the wisdom that only maturity and experience can impart. One such lady is dear Kate Armitage who at eighty-four years old, takes care of people in the village of Topsham. I will always be grateful for the support she gave my sister who was encountering the relentless effects of anorexia. As Kate walks by, there is a brisk skip in her step and her cheerful face lights up to greet passersby in the small village. With twinkling eyes and a sharply perceptive mind, she is genuinely concerned for other people's well-being. I hope, as I age myself, I will exhibit those qualities that she unquestioningly demonstrated. I look forward to seeing Kate whenever I visit England. My sister and I believe that she is without doubt, an angel disguised as an elderly lady.

Another dear friend, who at eighty-seven years old walks around the village in her high heels and pretty auburn colored hair, is a petite lady, always meticulously and beautifully dressed. Jane loves making tea whenever she has visitors; her curiosity and interest in numerous activities maintains the soft beauty in her face. A bright and elegant woman who traveled the world in her younger years, and is now writing fascinating stories about journeys through India

My intelligent mother-in-law Margaret Mills, has overcome numerous challenges in life through strength and courage; she continues to be a loving human being at eighty-four years old. I'm very grateful for her presence in my life and amazed at the way she copes so graciously, with a great deal of physical pain and the diminished capability of her eyesight.

Any pre-conceived ideas of 'sweet little old ladies' have been replaced by first-hand knowledge of strong, impressive and spirited women!

A dear friend when writing about her own parents wrote this recently: *"I feel like I am taking notes for my own future, on how to become and remain pliable, flexible and soft in the midst of all the losses, because I think that this is the secret. It is so hard to let go when we hold on so tight"*.

Margaret Mills, my mother-in-law as a young girl at University

Margaret Mills in 2007

116

Laughter

With a noticeable desire to entertain and *be* entertained, a flamboyant ninety-two year old lady was astonishingly lively in her social gallivanting. Having lived lavishly, even now her days continued to be filled with a luxurious pursuit of amusement. While helping her to write and edit an address book, and determined to fill it with high-flying names, she was extraordinarily adamant that I write the words *Viscountess* instead of a mere name. Intent on impressing anyone and everyone, she highlighted and emphasized her sparse connections with persons of *"title"*. This odd claim for self-esteem seemed pitiable.

A person may become a little self-absorbed with vainglorious aspirations and I wanted to believe that there was a little more to her character than what she had chosen to demonstrate to me.

Fighting her ageing process with ferocity, she was not taking it very gracefully. With recently failing sight and the support of a stick for aching knees, there were bitter outbursts of resentment. Temper tantrums undisguised and expressed through a hardened and shrinking face caused her husband to cower with dread at each caustic word.

The arrival in their household of a caregiver, companion and driver was supposed to be a gift from a loving son to assist his parents. Alas, her hostility grew to magnified proportions when she saw that the caregiver, who was forty years younger, represented *her* own lost youth. With undisguised fury over an ageing body, and in her view the irretrievable loss of good looks, she coveted youth in others. Surely if a person has fully valued each moment of their own life, they can have no desire to go back in time and retrieve misplaced treasures? She had possibly failed to appreciate the precious gift of youth when it was bountiful; had she squandered it?

One sunny morning while being driven into the nearby town, this feisty lady, as always, insisted on sitting in the front seat while her husband meekly sat in the back. This front seat position enabled her to be vigilant with the driver. The jaded driver looked wistfully out of the car window and was spontaneously drawn by the sight of two elderly ladies heartily laughing. Their faces were bright with animated enjoyment, as they stood surrounded by warm joyful light; their unabashed presence across the street was a magnet. Unashamed, the driver stared at them, totally absorbed and even uplifted by their merriment. A breath of life!

What had caused a few very privileged and elderly ladies to feel so deprived of contentment, whilst many hardworking women from the working classes expressed a vivacious lust for life, as well as being exceptionally kind and caring.

I've never quite known where I fit into the English class system because I carry the genes of my heritage in the form of my great grandparents. Sabine Baring-Gould came from the privileged classes, whereas his beautiful wife Grace, with whom he fell deeply in love when she was only sixteen years old, was a mill worker's daughter. Though antagonizing his whole family by this 'conduct', he remained true to his heart and Grace was sent to be schooled in the art of 'proper behavior and speech'. They had a long and happy marriage producing fourteen children. I heard that Bernard Shaw, who was a friend of my great grandfather, based his story *Pygmalion* on my great grandparents.

I am thrilled with my heritage from Grace who came from a working class background; I am a little uneasy with my legacy from the 'blue blooded' throng.

Those two smiling ladies certainly tossed life and laughter onto people's soul that day and without realizing it, they reached out to me on that sunny afternoon in November, because I was the wistful driver.

"Laughter is the shortest distance between two people"

~Victor Borge

Rita and Paddy

Their hearts' overflowed with generosity. After the harsh challenges of early childhood, Rita at age six, and her two brothers were sent to Dr. Bernardo's home for orphaned children where they faced and endured even more bleak ordeals. Having parents who were not able to care for their three children, the siblings were separated and alienated, only reuniting again after twelve long years. It was during World War Two and the children were in constant anxiety; bombs were hitting buildings and there were often times of darkness where no electricity was on hand. This was *home* and it was not a safe environment.

Rita was moved from location to location within the organization; the absence of stability or consistency during her twelve years at the Bernados' homes made a young child unsure of the world around her. Obligated to work at the age of eight, she began cleaning shoes and taking care of younger children – obligatory duties. Rita was often made to stand up all night on a landing as punishment for defying one of the strict and unreasonable regulations. Aged eighteen, a relieved Rita finally left Dr. Bernado's home and embarked on a life of service, which was being a servant in that era, as she had been trained to do.

Rita, a spirited woman in her seventies, had spent a lifetime running around at the beck and call of her employers over the last few decades. Now retired from service, she took care of dogs while the owners were away on vacation or weekends. The local residents in the village had every reason to trust Rita and Paddy with their beloved pets; the warm-hearted couple adored dogs and treated them as affectionately as though they were their own. The dogs were given love and lots of walks and were eager to see this couple again and again and again. On my numerous visits to their cozy home, the dogs would show visible signs of contentment. Climbing up on Paddy's lap, they appeared to be smiling.

Yes, Rita spent her life working hard for those who didn't always treat her with respect or appreciation. *Lovely Rita*, a seventy three year old woman with a wonderful sense of humor, a true heart of gold and a missing front tooth, started out in life with so little. She now has riches of the soul;

sapphires sparkling though her eyes and a laugh that generously sprinkles diamonds on all who meet her.

Others may have begun life with grand advantages and opportunities, and yet end their lives emotionally bankrupt. I wonder what makes a person open their heart to life and to *love their neighbor* in spite of great hardship. While others who have the gift of a comfortable upbringing, may grow to be impoverished and embittered, in their heart.

When visiting Paddy and Rita, I was met with a friendly welcome and homemade apple pie to eat - tea, coffee and ginger beer were offered with warm generosity. Incorporated in all this delicious fare was the comfort and laughter they emanated. Food for the soul! One could taste all those caring ingredients in Rita's apple pie while Paddy's rippling mirth brightened my day.

Walking along the pretty canal and visiting this couple was a ten-minute stroll through the village. Their simple home was a palace to me during that difficult time. There are angels in disguise in this world. It may not always be easy to see them but one can certainly sense their presence.

Thank you Rita and Paddy - for the wonderful apple pie and laughter.

The Evolved
Human Being

The fallacy that mankind is a superior species, dismays me. There's a strong belief too, that the lives of animals have no apparent value except for their usefulness in the human world.

An exceptionally graphic news report aired in 2004, where disgusting real life pictures were revealed – pictures that should surely move the *elevated* and civilized human to tears.

How do I begin to describe this despicable act carried out by mankind? An act that I watched in its full and detailed depravity. Nothing was left to the imagination. An act performed by a nation that holds the sacredness of religion and prayer, as an integral part of daily life.

This act is called *bear baiting*.

The British, while 'enlightening' other countries in the colonial era, were initially responsible for introducing this savage sport. Now according to a recent documentary, it continues as a recreational and popular pastime in Pakistan. People pay money to watch the show. The audience, organizers

125

and clearly the consenting authorities, appear to relish this sadistic performance. It's entertainment.

Vicious and hungry dogs are released to set upon a bear who has had all his or her teeth bashed out and every claw pulled out. Humans train the dogs to attack and kill their quarry, on command. A metal ring is placed through the bear's nose, after which the broken and defenseless prisoner is pulled into the showground. The bear is literally dragged into the arena by three men, and at every inch this resisting creature seems to plead for mercy, while its nose bleeds and its mouth emits white frantic froth. Fear glazes in the bear's eyes as dogs tear it to pieces.

Without any realistic hope of escape, I saw the lamentable bear trying to run from the dogs as they chased and pounced. A man, holding the unfortunate animal on a strong rope, gave the dogs' easier access to tear the bear to pieces.

This *amusing* game is paused every three minutes so that the audience can savor the view. They did not want the object of their amusement to die too quickly; otherwise the performance would be too brief! It was a lucrative venture.

Sickened at the memory of that documentary *and* at the savagery of human nature, the image of that helpless bear

126

disturbs me and should indeed upset anyone. The pain these bears endure and the hideous lust displayed in the gloating human faces gathered around the arena – continues to shock me. When did mankind lose its humanity? Was it ever there? Have we as humans squandered an opportunity to rise towards wisdom, compassion and spiritual awareness? After all, humans have been given the gift of consciousness, conscience and discernment. Animals kill for food and survival; humans appear to kill for fun and greed. Has the gift of discernment been discarded?

The unconditional love that is shown so often by animals reveals an evolved spirit - in my opinion.

"We are all connected;

To each other, biologically.

To the earth, chemically.

To the rest of the universe atomically."

Neil deGrasse Tyson

Diana

I will never forget the morning Princess Diana died.

Shocked and numbed along with most of the world, I felt compelled to join the thousands of people queuing up all over England, to write a few words of remembrance in books, considerately placed around the country. Mum was in hospital at that time, so my sister and I went to the quiet chapel inside the hospital to write our words of remembrance and in doing so, expressed our profound sadness at the loss. I was grateful to have a quiet setting so I could pay tribute to Diana and write my own personal words of reverence to an extraordinary woman.

People were pouring their hearts out, it was real, it was authentic and it was unforgettable. We lost a bright light in this world; a remarkable woman.

The Nation watched her funeral with gravity as tears of sadness flowed from a country in mourning. The world listened to the awe-inspiring song by Elton John, and the poignant words that poured from her brother's heart.

Diana's life ignited a spark of hope in people's hearts; her death left people stunned, her legacy is timeless. Her kindness touched thousands of ordinary human beings.

I wrote the following story one year before Diana died:

'Laughing fondly, I opened the newspaper to see yet another picture of Diana; her eyes were peeking over the surgical mask in a hospital operating room. She was on front-page news again – but the fact that she was totally loyal, devoted and committed to her crusade of caring for ordinary people was a detail that was disregarded and overlooked by ravenous reporters.

She had quietly slipped out of Buckingham Palace one night, as she had done on many nights, without the media ever knowing.

Ailing people were comforted by these surprise and gentle visits. Her interest in reassuring the sick was an aspiration instigated by empathy and a deep wish to bring comfort to people who were suffering. It was her own need and compassionate desire to help. And she did help.'

While wishing to educate herself by being part of a surgical team, someone had cunningly taken a photo, which unsurprisingly made front-page news. Attending a surgical procedure would broaden her sense of empathy for those who had undergone major surgery. Doing exactly what she genuinely believed in - she continued to attract unwanted media attention.

Diana faced constant envy and criticism and I found it hard to understand the spiteful comments emerging from people who seemed embittered in their own life. Those with tenderness and innocence in their heart - loved Diana.

Diana didn't always conform to conventional concepts; her intent was to care and to be concerned about the well-being of ordinary people. According to stiff and outdated rules, perhaps she didn't 'behave as a Royal should behave' - she hugged people! In the eyes of decent people however, Diana exemplified nobility, dignity and above all a generous spirit.

What callous person would disapprove of these actions and in so doing cause her so much pain.'

Diana was, and still *is* a presence emanating goodness. She is irreplaceable. She gave humanity a spark of hope. Her legacy is immortal.

What a richer world this would have been had Diana lived to be Queen – A Queen of Hearts.

"If we have no peace,
It is because we have forgotten
That we belong to each other"

Mother Teresa

Prince Harry

"I'm doing what my mother would want me to do"

Prince Harry

He was in Africa spending some time at an orphanage where most of the children's parents' had already died of aids; these children were HIV positive.

With an earnest wish to support his mother's work, he said that 'he could never take over her work, nobody could, but he could help'. While he was holding an African baby in his arms, I watched the documentary with interest, and saw how tenderly this young man stroked her tiny face - comforting a small human being with heartfelt kindness. As she lay quietly in his arms her big bright eyes made an indelible impact on me.

Shockingly, her stepfather had raped the ten-month-old baby girl because the local medicine man had apparently told him that this was how to purify the child of sickness. Looking at those blinking innocent eyes, I was overwhelmed at the tragedy of a helpless human being who couldn't even speak yet. A baby who couldn't possibly comprehend what had been done to her. A very young human being had been cruelly exposed to the unscrupulous and malicious self-indulgence of the human adult in all its corruption. This small child lay peacefully in Harry's arms, absorbing the love and warmth being offered. I saw the face of Diana in her son. The tender compassion and authenticity of caring was expressed in this quiet, strong face. Harry had just turned twenty years old.

It was a short documentary that received very little media attention.

The very next day, a newspaper columnist, neglecting to comment on the sad plight of the children had chosen instead to launch a verbal and personal assault on the Prince - cynically implying that this was a 'mere photo opportunity'. I was surprised at the lack of awareness shown towards an obvious humanitarian concern and choosing instead, to demean a benevolent project. Have some humans lost their soul?

The documentary was a factual endeavor to bring attention to these abused children.

Knowing Diana's sons will continue her work because they *are* her sons, gives me a sense of gratitude.

During that same week the sensational and non-stop media coverage focused on a few young men loudly protesting against the proposed ban on fox hunting. Five of these boys crept stealthily into the outer chambers and stormed into the inner sanctum of Parliament, generating chaos. The obvious lack of security was causing a lot of commotion. Pictures of these so called 'heroes' with their important crusade of promoting brutal fox hunting, were splashed all over the newspapers. These brazen young men were outraged that *their* British tradition was about to be curtailed - they were fighting to uphold British society! They were crusading passionately to maintain the continuance of fox hunting. It was broadcasted around as 'patriotism' in all its glory. Banning their beloved sport they said pompously, 'would compromise the democracy of their country'. The five well-heeled youths, were not willing to allow the majority of voters who were ordinary animal loving people – to fight for animal welfare. Faces glowing with arrogant defiance, they seemed enormously pleased with themselves.

For many years, animal loving citizens considered fox hunting to be a cruel sport and had been lobbying to ban it. A large group of hounds, chase an exhausted fox until they catch and tear it to pieces while brightly costumed humans riding on horses, seem exhilarated and feel they have cause to celebrate – a job well done! Fox hunting is clearly a sport for those who have the time, the staff *and* the costume. Personally I feel this is an outdated tradition that needs to be reviewed.

I was beset by the opposing aspirations of these young men in their twenties. One who was quietly concerned about poverty and illness in Africa. The others – noisy and self-righteously 'patriotic'. Both hoping to make their crusade public.

Compassion can't be faked. No amount of charitable tea parties in the midst of ladies with fashionable hats can compare to the meaningful authenticity of real awareness and caring. To know another's pain is to feel it and have the courage to feel *for* them. The inability to truly sense the pain in others often results in a need to deride those who can.

Diana *felt* the pain of others.

Wild Tai Chi

Like a waterfall bubbling, sizzling and pounding onto the big rocks, the river was flowing wildly that morning in Tavistock, a little village near Dartmoor. This momentary and untamed vision was vitalizing. Up until now I'd just seen the serenity of this lovely river.

As the impassioned water flowed wildly on its journey, I glimpsed someone through the trees; or was it just a movement? A man standing on a concrete wedge directly above the cascading spray was performing Tai Chi in tune with the rhythmic movement around him. In deference to this natural phenomenon, he seemed to be dancing with the exuberant river.

Not wanting to disturb a unique moment or intrude on his graceful movement, I peeped through the trees with a sense of awe. Then without reserve I came a little closer to watch this lively dance on the rocks. The artistic meditator glanced at me and to my relief, continued without interruption. I acknowledged this soulful dance to the river, and walked away.

I had been privy to a beautiful moment; a rare and precious moment.

Hot Cocoa

This narrative was related to me by my mother. It is her perspective on these events. I also know that my own mother bore a lifelong resentment towards her own mother. I never knew my grandmother, so any judgment towards her, may be flawed. I know how reproachful and biased my mother could be towards others.

My maternal grandmother Florence Elvira Burr was considered to be beautiful and perhaps self-absorbed according to her daughter. Accustomed to and having been born into privileged society, Florence enjoyed the high life. Living life luxuriously in her youthful thirties with other British Nationals residing in Mexico City, she had material comforts that sustained a lifestyle of pleasure. Florence Elvira was not very happy when she left Mexico, along with many other British nationals. It had been her home for years.

Suddenly depleted of assets and possessions, Europeans were forced to abandon their wealth and leave Mexico. Without the lavish comforts and sparkling social life she was accustomed to, life for Elvira seemed dire after returning to

139

England, where the family settled in St. John's Wood, London with their two children. It was a relative who offered a home for the family. Elvira towed her small daughter along with her to film auditions – my glamorous grandmother hankered to be an actress. Or perhaps she was trying to earn a living.

In spite of her now relative dismal predicament of *scarcity,* she did, nevertheless, inherit a beautiful house in Axminster Devon, Highfield House, was left to her and my great grandmother, by a caring brother after he died during the looming shadow of World War Two.

There was someone coming in on a daily basis to clean the house; a cleaning lady in those days was often referred to as the '*charwoman*'. Florence perceived the cleaning lady not as an actual person but a useful commodity to be utilized as a kitchen appliance, according to my mother's narration. The 'charwoman' was allowed one cup of hot cocoa to warm her body in the harsh cold English winter of the 1930s'.

Times were uneasy. People were working hard for long hours and not earning much money. There was no welfare system in place yet. The English class system was glaringly evident, and a chasm between rich and poor was embarrassingly noticeable. The working classes were beset

140

with tough times - the privileged classes, by all accounts, still managed to eat and live well.

As a child, my mother felt that she had an inherent ability to appreciate and seek out the essential qualities in people and animals. On occasions I saw this very quality in her during my growing years. She claimed to see merit and beauty in each person and reached out to life with understanding - be it human, animal or flower. My mother noticed that the cleaning lady's cocoa was made with boiling water, without any milk being added. Milk seemed to be a luxury, banned for those who worked in menial labor.

At twelve years old, Mum said that would find some creamy milk and leave it out for the charwoman to put in her cocoa. She even gave this thin, quiet lady an egg to take home. Mum said that it gave her pleasure in knowing that someone had felt the hand of warmth in their life. When an egg disappeared, Florence Elvira was furious, even accusing the unfortunate charwoman of stealing it. Mum was sharply reprimanded for giving Martha an egg – nevertheless my mother boldly continued to provide the cleaning lady with creamy milk and an occasional egg. Florence said: *"Those type of people don't need milk in their cocoa"*.

Without making any distinction between herself and 'these people' – Mum apparently felt that to be human was a shared feature, no matter what your status at birth or monetary standing. She was concerned for the skinny lady who quietly worked hard to clean a big house, and who indeed had very little material comfort to go home to. Mum's gesture was a simple attempt to recognize and ease the predicament of another human being. Mum's compassion burst through like a blossoming flower and she wanted to share whatever she had.

My mother said that she grew up a lonely child. Reaching out to people, animals, flowers and trees gave her solace; she communed with nature and adored her beloved Dartmoor in Devon, the south of England. This I know to be true about my mother and I share in that solace of nature myself. Mum's only sibling and the person who truly gave her affection, she said, was John, her older brother, who sadly died in a motorbike accident at age sixteen. Mum sought out love in her own way after that and was overjoyed to find a little rabbit wandering in a field nearby; something to love and cuddle. Knowing that the rabbit would not be accepted as an adored pet, she thought it better to hide the warm fluffy animal in the back garden where she secretly took care of it for three weeks, until it was discovered. Unbeknownst to Mum, my grandmother got rid of *it*. In Florence's mind, the rabbit was a nuisance when in fact, the rabbit was Mum's best friend and confidant at that time. I understand this sentiment myself, because as a child my trusted friends were a cat and a dog who listened lovingly to my heartfelt troubles.

Coincidentally my paternal grandmother also lost her fortune during the great depression of the 1930s'. As a child I was told of the shocking event when my grandmother (Diana Amelia Baring-Gould) fainted in the bank after hearing the news that her assets had dissolved into thin air. Both my father and mother had endured the painful experience of growing up with parents who coped with difficulty after the sudden loss of their assets. I myself grew up in modestly unpretentious surroundings, with the added knowledge that I have grandparents on both sides who were, at one time, in possession of wealth and status.

I have a particular inclination to write about the disparity often involved within the British class system and I sense an inherent need to bridge that division. Admittedly nowadays, the chasm is influenced by wealth more than lineage – but a division persists. I wonder whether any society will ever see unity, respect and equality as a worthy objective.

I would like to think that my mother's narration has value. I would have loved to have met her mother, my grandmother, with my own thoughts and feelings about someone in my bloodline. Mum did have a tendency sometimes to applaud herself, while convincingly blaming or scapegoating other people.

"Our task must be to free ourselves
By widening our circle of compassion
To embrace all living creatures
And the whole of nature and its beauty"

Albert Einstein

Birdsong

"Listening to bird songs,
I can't help but feel
The beauty of their souls"

HAIKU - By Atmo Ram

Sweet chirping voices building up to an orchestra amongst the trees are sounds that have enthralled mankind for centuries, even consoling people during times of angst and despair.

Staring dejectedly through a kitchen window one afternoon, I kept hearing a distant flute like sound that persevered and eventually penetrated my lonely thoughts. Puzzled by this insistent sound, I saw one gallant little bird chirping loudly outside the window. Snapping abruptly out of my musing I noticed all the pretty birds singing heartily in the garden. Immersed in their lovely songs, I looked with tenderness at tiny fragile bodies darting energetically around the garden; they seemed to demand one's attention out of pure compassion. How can one not be filled with gentle laughter as colorful birds flit amongst trees?

Do people surround themselves with numbness? Have we lost touch with the most beautiful way of communicating with life, with each other and with all of nature?

Twelve years before, while living in San Diego and trying to see my way through 'life's drama', little birds were alighting and twittering boldly on the table in front of me. Sitting at the small wooden table in an enchantingly serene café surrounded by green leafy trees, I heard bright chirping sounds. The present and pure moment of time was unexpectedly and comfortingly apparent. Freed from the lure of anxiety, I felt at peace again and some unresolved concerns mysteriously fell into place that very afternoon.

Such tiny little beings bring joy to mankind. A reminder to savor and relax into the moment; a signal too that answers are not found through anxiety and worry. I hope that we as humans will not totally forget how to feel connected with all of life. I am grateful for those persistent stimuli.

"Birds outside my cabin window,

singing love songs

to the morning rain"

HAIKU - By Atmo Ram

There is a Human Being

After my brother sold me his little black Ford Fiesta car, which I named 'Mox' (the name on the number plate), I began exploring the countryside while re-visiting and savoring scenery that had been part of my growing years in Devon and Dorset. *Mox* proved to be a sturdy little vehicle that became a treasured companion on these jaunts, never failing to start her engine and never complaining at the amount of driving we did. *Mox* was quite old and statistically didn't have much life left, but 'she' stood by me with stoic loyalty. Actually we were a trio – *Mox*, the camera and myself.

Feeling gripped by the exploration of photography, I wanted to capture some striking English scenery. Paradoxically, I'd never been impassioned with photography until this moment, though for the last twenty years there were numerous opportunities to take fantastic photos in a variety of exotic countries, and yet, in those days, I firmly believed that the photograph was in my heart and not on paper. It was different now where I hungered after this newly discovered venture. Gazing at the countryside with a specific eye to a potential and timeless embodiment of the majesty around me, I clicked the camera with childlike delight. My heart danced at images captured in a photo and a deeper understanding for my father arose, because he had been engrossed in the excitement of photography himself. Dad developed and printed the photos he took while living in Africa and his camera never seemed to leave his side. I now had a renewed appreciation of that driving passion for the art of photography. I experience that same vibrant enthusiasm that my father must have felt throughout his life.

On one of those days of driving around, I felt weary. Those coastal spots of particular beauty were now invaded by overcrowded parking lots and robotic machines that required exact change. Big brash holiday camps had been built around a stunning wild cove called Ladram Bay. An increasing struggle just to access those breathtaking scenes was made tough for anyone seeking out quiet and beautiful landscapes, which were being made accessible for crowds of fun loving tourists. Ladram Bay was untouched by human 'progress' two decades before, whereas now it seemed grueling to navigate through all the obstructions in the newly built profiteering paraphernalia of this modern holiday camp.

Imagine my surprise when I pulled into the picturesque seaside town of Sidmouth, hoping to photograph the Jurassic and Triassic beauty of the Devonshire coast, I found a small parking lot close to the pebbly beach. A friendly elderly man appeared in the window of a wooden hut and just like in the 'old days', he expressed a genuinely welcoming smile as he handed me a ticket to park. I wanted to savor that moment because a real person and a good-humored face was a rare occurrence. I miss a human voice in this modern age of parking machines. I wonder how much longer this small privately owned haven with a *real* attendant would be allowed to stay, before the parking corporations take over and swallow it in their belly of greed and exploitation. The stress of finding exact change for those faceless machines and the pressure of knowing you have to return by a specific time for fear of being penalized by an outlandish fine, imparts yet another aspect of tension in this modern existence.

This friendly human assured me that I can pay for my ticket to cover an hour of parking; and if I exceeded the hour any additional fee could be simply and easily paid on departure. There was no robotic punishment for anyone whose ticket expired and consequently, I felt relaxed while meandering around the sandy beach. The man in the wooden hut said with warm kindliness: *"You can pay as you go out if your ticket expires"*. What a sense of relief to hear those words and what a surprise to have found this oasis.

Thank you Sidmouth!

Car park attendant, Mick Vaughan

I'm 55

I turned fifty-five years old – yes, old! How did that happen?

Echoes of a limited future reverberate loudly. Will I ever find a job now? When will the sagging wrinkles appear? At age fifty-four my whole life was ahead; now at fifty-five it's a different story – I'm 'over the hill'.

People of my age talk about pensions, retirement and grandchildren. I will get used to that I'm sure but for now, it feels alarming.

On grim days, while hearing friends talking about grandchildren, a sense of my own perceived 'failure' is magnified - wishing that I, too, had children and grandchildren to play with and share stories of their growing years. A rosy vision of grandchildren who love you no matter how grey and wrinkled you become seems so appealing. On more joyful days, I'm enchanted and thrilled at those very grandparent-narratives from friends. With the practical knowledge that my life abruptly took a different path after my daughter died.

While walking by some neat, secure and well-heeled houses during my fifty-fifth year, I felt the breath of air from my mother and in that moment, knew that I had tried to live a life true to my heart and without any wish to hurt others along the way. Being a *free spirit* may be imprudent, but nevertheless demands courage and commitment, particularly when you reach age fifty-five! Maybe being a free spirit was not a choice but the path I found myself walking in life.

There is great wisdom in generating a secure material life without needing to surrender the bright light of authenticity in the process; but who would wish to be cooped up in a safe secure box or to live a life of discontent at the expense of forfeiting one's unique and precious path in life?

Each choice has its price as well as reward. Could I have lived happily when sacrificing my soul in order to have a comfortable pension?

I'm reminded of my mother's spirit – a mixture of courage, foolishness, emotion, impulsiveness and joy. Maybe I was never brought up to be practical.

Seagulls
and Squirrels

Echoes of the invigorating ocean in winter are indelibly linked to the sound of seagulls as recollections of days on the coast of Dorset wash over me. I am profoundly fond of the sound of seagulls.

That particular January day, during an outing to buy fish at the local fishmonger on the Devon coast, a pleasurable buoyancy rippled through my spirit when the sound of copious seagulls came swirling around white foamed waves.

On commenting on the wonder of these sounds, an abrupt response reverberated from the elderly lady I was taking care of for two weeks: *"They are dirty horrible things,"* she said brusquely.

A slightly humorous but sad emotion struck me at that moment, as a soundless rejoinder was the only form of response I could rally.

Hoping to cheer up this stern lady, I later pointed out some adorable squirrels amongst the trees around her lush home. Little faces bobbing around green leaves filled me with laughter and delight as they rushed around with food storage preparations for the coming winter months: *"They are nothing but rats; tree rats that should be poisoned!"* she said.

With a rigid voice and an overcast face, she appeared wholly untouched by the delights of nature. A dull echo of self-pity seemed the only motivation in her insular world.

Though disappointed at a wide-ranging human inclination to shut out the bright stimulation of life's splendors, it seems that the enchanted voices of nature are only accessible to those who *see* and hear them.

Bringing joy into the life of an elderly lady while hoping that the pleasure of past memories would swirl to the surface, I was convinced there would be moments of laughter and smiles for us both.

Perhaps my desires were idealistic. Somewhere in this lady's life journey, she had abandoned the spark of genuine pleasure. Maybe in a frozen memory, these creatures had caused some distress in her past and the residue of acrimony was set in stone.

There's a cultural indentation in the British character to be perceived as non-sentimental and frostily 'matter-of-fact' while in the process, forsaking the human experience to feel bliss as well as sorrow.

However cynical, dispassionate or even frozen some people may become, there persists the glorious sense of elation when embracing our proximity to the unforgettable and infinite language of nature; the sounds and sights of which *will* find a way to penetrate even the most insensate individuals. Perhaps, in such blessed moments of recognition, gratitude triumphs over bitterness and inner peace emerges.

Gratitude is an art of painting adversity
into a lovely picture. ~

Kak Sri

When ....

'When this bottle of scent is finished, I will end the relationship'.

Afraid to imagine that love could last, at the age of seventeen those were the words I repeated to myself after meeting eighteen-year-old Felix, so many years ago.

An outward show of strength is often, in reality, the trepidation of love or the fear of losing love. Or perhaps it's the apprehension of potential rejection in the future, or maybe just a desire to feel safe by being one step ahead of circumstances. An illusion of safety can be compelling.

Assuming that the vision of true and eternal love could possibly be a mere fantasy and for that reason come to a raw ending, I was definitely afraid of trusting my heart to the capricious hand of fate. At the young age of eighteen I was already trying to protect myself from hurt and rejection. Not having to face the unknown mystery of an evolving relationship seemed to be a clever choice at the time.

Unthreatened by vulnerability gives one a misconception of being unshakable.

Am I part of a culture that fears giving one's heart to life and love? Is receptivity and innocence such a dreadful prospect and are we a society of people who need to calculate our actions in order to protect heartfelt feelings? Are we really meant to pretend we are strong and is it considered clever to be 'ahead of the game' when it comes to genuine feelings? This must be an age-old dilemma and it saddens me to think in my own young eighteen year old life, I needed to *end* something simply because I was afraid the other person will do it before me.

Now years' later, with the added knowledge that age, experience and a little more understanding brings to us all – it's clear that to truly value *love*, one has to be open to grief and loss. By shutting out pain, we shut out love.

The mystery of life will always hold uncertainty, but as the saying goes:

'It's better to have loved and lost,
than never to have loved'!

"I'm Passionate about Staying Alive"

"Tears of Joy are like summer raindrops, pierced by sunbeams"

Hosea Ballou

These words came from a beautiful lady with big smiling eyes who spoke about her encounter with breast cancer and the wholehearted effort to cure this condition. With the driving force of someone who is determined not to give up the fight for life, she spoke with elation and motivation. She had so much to live for, as anyone could see when her twenty-year-old son stood at her side.

Feelings of self-pity in my own life vanished in that moment. I had been running into numerous challenges and in moments of despondency, lacked the impetus to see a way forward while at the same time asking *why* wonderful and irreplaceable people who had succeeded in their lives, contracted terminal disease and died. I couldn't understand the hand of providence as I asked myself –

'*Why* ......*a wonderful lady called Linda died of ovarian cancer at age fifty-two; Linda had a stable job, two beautiful teenage children – she and her husband had spent a lifetime working hard and now owned a lovely house overlooking the ocean near Seattle; they were ready for a well-deserved retirement – together*'.

He was a very lonely husband when she died.

'*Why*... *a stunning and intelligent twenty year old girl in Switzerland had to cope with cancer for the past three years*' –

'*Why*... *a friend's vibrant twelve year old son had to die within six months of discovering a tumor in his abdomen*'

They all had *so* much to live for!

When sadness transmutes into depression and despair becomes self-pity, we find ourselves burdened by a heavy cloud of desolation. An overflowing gratitude mercifully emerges when a window of inspiration opens to illuminate the disconsolate heart once again. The encounter with this motivated lady, fighting for her life in such a dignified and loving way, brought clarity and fresh hope - to me. I found myself saying: *"I'm passionate about staying alive too"*

A deep understanding and an unspoken truth became apparent – we simply can't know the *why* of our existence and all it encompasses. Trusting each step in this mortal embodiment is the only path of consciousness that I can think of at this moment.

"I don't believe that people
are looking for the meaning of life
as much as they are looking for
the experience of being alive"

Joseph Campbell

Snapshots of.............

A snapshot can leave an indelible and timeless imprint where a moment in time becomes truly eternal and the infinity of an instant is time honored.

A Lovely Family

Four members of a truly close family who heartfully share the character and essence of their unified spirit, invite others into the soul of their unanimity. I was immediately immersed in a *'flower garden'* where each unique multihued fragrance merges into the harmony of a family. A 'flower garden' that blooms with a vital energy of life.

Sandy-haired Marcus plays the piano, sings Beatles songs and drums with a rapt intensity, while conveying all the dedication of a gifted adult.

Radiating an insightful and genuine sincerity, Lottie plays the piano with dancing hands; she drums with a sunbeam in her smile and glides around the house in a flowery skirt while glowing with the playful joy of youth. Ingrid's gently beautiful face and expressive eyes reflect the thoughtful and highly intelligent mother who deeply cares about her family *and* humankind. John's melodious voice, scholarly mind and quiet strength reflect a father and human being who truly *hears* what people are saying.

The group of four invited me into their world for an unforgettable hour – a music studio where they melt in unison to the music played by these gifted teenagers. Yes it was a mere snapshot and a single moment of intersecting lives, and yet it was *so* much more! For someone like me, who often feels excluded and an outsider, I felt immensely valued by being *included* in a family unit.

Priscilla

Her enchanting garden was a special treat on route to the village shop. In a little world of its own, flowers sprinkled with pretty seashells were bursting with life. A petite wooden bench was decoratively strewn with pears and sunflower heads; I imagined that fairies came fluttering around the place. Any mortal passerby was sure to be immersed in the charm and delight of this sweet patch.

Wearing a pale pink top and flowered skirt, Priscilla pottered around her flowers and I'm sure they communed in the most amiable way. Wearing sparkly flip flop sandals, she exuded an air of uncomplicated enjoyment, while a rosy face and white hair gave her the appearance of a character straight from one of my childhood nursery rhymes - a good fairy whose garden brings pleasure to anyone who happens to walk by.

Doris

She opened her blue eyes and smiled when I told her about the small bright colored bird who had sat quietly in my hand that sunny afternoon in June. Doris died that night and I like to believe the little bird was an indication that this blue eyed lady's husband who had passed away ten years before, was now coming to meet her.

As Doris lay breathing her last breath of life, I sat quietly in another room when the lights flickered at eleven thirty that night and in that moment I knew Doris was flying away, just as the little bird had done in the afternoon.

Though sad to see her go, I knew that she was winging her way to a higher place. She was ninety-three years old. And I had only known Doris for one week as her caregiver.

Snapshots of people and incidents we all encounter in the course of a lifetime bring color, warmth and drama into our individual world. These are just three snapshots that reveal personalities who knowingly or unknowingly opened the doors of their heart so that others may glimpse at the brightly lit spirit of another human being.

We all have qualities to share – sadly most humans shun their own unique and entrancing persona; as a result it's never revealed to others. What an enigma!

"*Enlightenment is intimacy with all things*"

Dogen

"Before death knocks on your door,
Share – whatsoever you have.
You can sing a beautiful song – sing it!
Share it.
You can paint a picture – paint!
Share it.
I have never come across a man
who has not much to share".

OSHO

The following pages are in memory

Of my mother

Elizabeth Maxwell-Batten

Fondly nick-named 'Emma'

174

A Celebration of our Mum's life

By Major Dominic Maxwell-Batten

Mum died on December 5ᵗʰ 2001.

It is a sad day, a sad time. We have lost our beloved mother. A wonderful and remarkable woman, an irreplaceable person.

Mourning has its place and is important, a gratitude for what has been, the grief of loss and the pain of missing. Above all is perhaps the uncertainty, the 'what *ifs'* of both past and future. I can't answer these 'what *ifs'*. I don't think anyone truly can. If there were a definite and catalogued answer there would be no scope for faith. Now, faith is something I can talk about. My mother had faith. Faith in God and Faith in others. A faith that guided her along life's path. The path she chose was that of generosity and caring. Mum had a huge capacity to care and would willingly give up whatever she had in the belief that it could help someone else. Putting others before herself and seeking out those in need was consistent throughout her life. And challenging convention where she perceived convention to be unjust or where it delivered inequality or hardship was merely the right thing to do in her eyes. Indeed, wherever convention supported self-indulgence and pomposity our mother found challenge. But judgments were never made. Mum would never judge another person, only offer to pick them up when they had fallen.

This lack of regard for convention often found our mother misunderstood. All through our childhood my siblings and I found children from less happy homes welcomed to share in our Mum's love and given the warmth of a home. Mum cared for these children and tried to ease their destitution. Her life was largely devoted to helping them and their families in whatever way she was able. Driven by a need to give love to those children who had none. Another love was for animals and steadily their numbers in our household grew. Strays of all shapes and sizes were welcomed into our home and given love and care and food.

Part of the human condition is imperfection. After all there could be no perfection without imperfection and our mother as all people had her faults but none that seemed to matter. Mum loved the countryside and especially Dartmoor. Nothing could have been more indulgent for our Mum than to walk through rabbit trodden summer fields, rich with buttercups and cowslips, soaking in the purity of nature.

If I were asked to do the impossible and to sum up our Mum in a few thoughts I should have to say that her love for us has made us strong and taught us compassion. That her sense of humor, curiosity and thirst for knowledge inspired us all. Her poetry and storytelling intrigued us. Her courage protected us. But above all her generosity, to family and to all those Mum saw as needy was her greatest gift.

Mum there are many who love you but none more than your devoted family. We will miss you but we are comforted in the knowledge that we will be together again.

My brother Dominic with his beloved dog, Henry

This enchanting tree is rooted on the grounds of what used to Shute School for girls near Axminster in Devon. My Mother attended the school in 1935, and I can't help feeling she saw and felt the magnificence of this historic and beautiful tree.

179

Dad

My Mother

She didn't make us clean our teeth or come home *or* even go to bed at a specific time; nor did she find it necessary to have set meal schedules – we ate when we were hungry. That simply made sense on a very instinctive level.

As we were growing up, my mother didn't always remember to wash or iron our clothes for school, my siblings and myself were spontaneously motivated to do it ourselves if we wished to look clean and well turned out. When she suddenly decided to paint pictures, equipped with a newly purchased easel, paintbrushes and canvas from the local second hand shop, she became absorbed in the pursuit of art. Fervently painting dramatic and sweeping pictures while smoking black Russian cigarettes, she was clearly immersed in her project. I walked through our front door one afternoon to see clouds of smoke circling above an easel. I knew Mum was completely absorbed in her latest impulse, or obsession perhaps, and we naturally found our own way to keep up with practical issues, like getting something to eat and going to school.

While living at 'Woodlands', our beautiful home in Dorset, I would sunbathe on the windowsill watching to see if anyone came to our door. Mum, nowhere to be seen, was usually sleeping amongst the bluebells and hazel trees somewhere in the five-acre dwelling. Still recuperating from the severe effect of having typhoid, contracted in East Africa, the soothing haven amongst sweet smelling bluebells was restoring her vitality in many ways.

Were we all free spirits or was that the alluring pretext of my mother? Nobody seemed to know where the other was or what he or she was doing; having said that, my Mother said that she had an intuitive ability to know if her children needed her, or whether they were in trouble.

Playing alone in a river one morning in Lyme Regis, the pretty seaside village in Dorset, I was engrossed in splashing amongst the pebbles when my foot slipped on some broken glass, and was painfully slit open. Within ten minutes my mother appeared in the car and took me to the local cottage hospital where the gash was stitched up. Perhaps she knew the places I liked to visit; she definitely knew that I was in trouble. Neither of us thought that it was an unusual occurrence; we naturally assumed there was a non-verbal communiqué. Perhaps a concerned onlooker or neighbor had phoned my mother to let her know that her daughter was limping due to a bleeding foot.

My father, the more traditional parent, was in Africa with his government job during some of our childhood years. Though attempting to put practicality into effect in our family, my mother was the stronger character!

Mum *did* teach her children how to breathe in the fragrance of flowers, to laugh uncontrollably with joy and to feel the gentle breeze on our faces; Mum felt it was important to hear birds singing. She educated us to become aware of the unpredictable rhythm and beauty of nature She displayed these attributes herself and that is how we learnt. Feeling the ocean on our bodies, smelling the drying seaweed on rocks as the tide went out, hearing seagulls screeching for food, are lessons and memories imprinted in my soul.

She was not always sensible; in fact, I don't really think anyone could describe my mother as level-headed; nevertheless, she gave us the *pearl* that people often seek far and wide, which was to *feel* and live Life fully.

Many didn't understand her poetry. I like to think she was ahead of her time in a strangely mystical, supernatural way. Perhaps her poetry was far seeing.

Now as an adult I notice people, friends and acquaintances who were taught to clean their teeth, to eat at certain times and pay attention to practical issues so that it may have scarred their subtle senses. A childlike awe of life can become submerged in that process. People take anti-depressants and their innocence vanishes as they forfeit an innate ability to see birds in the sky, sit peacefully under a tree or bury their face in flowers – an ability to taste, feel and touch has frozen like a frost bitten limb with no sensation as people search for something that they already have, even paying money for therapy, workshops and psychoanalysis in a desperate longing to re-discover their own passion and authenticity. Did my mother give us the gift of 'non-conformity?

Some people may have felt we were neglected on those practical levels, and admittedly, I would have liked a little more assistance and attention to prudent issues as I was growing up. Practical issues, on the other hand, come and go and can even become a guarded and unhealthy clinging to security.

I walked through the gate into the front garden at *'The Shrubbery'* one warm sunny afternoon and saw that Mum was asleep in the deck chair next to her enchanting frog pond. She cherished that little pond which was contained in an old wooden whiskey barrel. Mum spent summer afternoons watching the frogs climbing out to look around; it stirred her childlike excitement.

Her soft, unwrinkled face was peaceful as she lay there sleeping – deeply tranquil, not even stirring or moving as I came through the gate.

She was certainly at peace with her surroundings on that sunny afternoon; it remains one of the many lasting memories I have of my mother.

"Death – the last sleep?
No, it is the final awakening"

~ Walter Scott

Her Last Days

"You're here, you're here," she said with a childlike smile that warmed my heart. Hurriedly bringing my luggage into the hospital after having just arrived from America, I dared not miss even a second of being with Mum.

Her blue eyes sparkled as I walked through the door of the hospital room where she lay; my sister was sitting close to her – helping Mum to eat a small spoon of yogurt.

I sat with her after that, not wanting to leave her side. That evening she sank into semi-consciousness and her blue eyes took on a familiar softness.

Every so often she jumped as though frightened, crying out in her sleep: *"Help" – help!"*

It worried me and it concerned me. I felt helpless. What was distressing her, I wondered? I held her hand and comforted her. She wasn't able to tell me what happened or why she was frightened. I could only soothe her each time she awoke. Next day I discovered what had occurred in the last few days. A ginger haired nurse had forced powdered medicines down her throat without mixing it with any liquid; it was not easy to swallow and mum choked. The nurse, who had been very edgy with Mum, seemed unable to express the gentle and loving receptivity towards people who are ill and frail, and it was clear that her heart was not in her work.

That same nurse grumbled at us for sitting around our dying mother in those last hours. She said that there were too many of us and instructed us to take turns when sitting with our mother. It seemed that we as a whole family were a nuisance to her. I wondered whether the nurse herself had a lonely and loveless life.

In spite of the disapproving looks, we all stayed together quietly sitting with our mother as she lay in a peaceful sleep. She didn't wake up. It was a rare moment where five children sat silently in unison – each conveying our individual goodbye. We did not feel any need to separate. It was a moment in time that was deeply sad; we each had our own thoughts and feelings as we sat *as one*. No words could describe the emotions we were experiencing, but the loving stillness that surrounded our tender sanctuary, said everything.

Within minutes of our Mum's death the same ginger haired nurse tried to hurry us all away so that she could '*get on with her work*'. We weren't permitted to sit silently and say our final goodbye in *our* way. I had felt that the moment of Mum's death was sacred and I needed to come to terms with what had just happened. The nurse was keen to get the bed ready for the next patient and she made no attempt to hide her impatience. With a face that revealed an imprisoned heart she had no sentiment for such a rare and consequential event. She attempted to steal *our* moment of love and our poignant farewell to a cherished human being. I often wonder to this day what caused this nurse to have relinquished her own feelings of sensitivity towards others. I felt aggrieved, I felt powerless and I felt abused by the nurse in a moment of profound and personal vulnerability.

I still have an ache in my heart when I think of Mum's last days; every fiber of my being wanted it to be different. I wanted her to be nurtured and loved in her final days and hours. But now, mostly I feel that my mother is free. I feel thankful in knowing that she is liberated from a painful and difficult body.

The day Mum died I noticed the breezy day outside. Leaves were fluttering in the windy air and I knew that she was dancing with the trees – her free spirit joyful and young again. The moon was deep purple that night, with a pink ring of soft cloud around it – she was close to us – her children. After that month I felt an immeasurable bond with my siblings, I didn't want to leave England. I returned to Seattle with a heavy heart.

I will always be grateful for the treasured friends that I came to know during the years I spent in Seattle but in this moment, I felt lonely. An unspoken connection with my siblings was deep-rooted and difficult to leave behind.

Mum, when she was young

A Poem by My Mother:

'The Philosophy of why I Write"

By Elizabeth Maxwell-Batten

Many people ask me why I write, why I like to write,

What reason?

That is a difficult question with an equally difficult answer.

Why do painters paint?

Musicians compose!

I believe beautiful music and beautiful paintings

are small chinks in the curtain that obscures heaven.

As I write maybe, maybe sometimes I can find that small chink

in the curtain, and if people look – still allowing themselves to

feel, I mean feel with their heart,

perhaps with their soul, they too may find this tiny chink.

I wish to share my joy;

Of a quiet sunset on a summer evening,

A small flower growing in a crevice of a barren cliff,

Moorland, with the scent of gorse and heather,

The heavy drone of a single bumblebee laden with honey,

The tangy smell of earth when the rain has newly fallen.

So many things – young beech leaves feeling their way

sensitively into the soft spring air,

with the haze of bluebells, at their feet.

Is this not a chink in Heaven's curtain?

It is a lonely thing not to share, a moment so exquisite in this sad world.

I know age now. I have looked it in the face; it has no place in humanity, only the world is holding age close.

I feel now that this is the fault of man, we still have beauty in the eye of seeing and hearing……… the earth is being made to grow old before the time.

The womb is shuddering under the burden of commerce.

Of what shall the womb give birth??

Monsters (?) – or the sons of God.

There again, does it matter sons and daughters of God, we are alone with the earth, with infinity, with the spark of the Spirit.

Let's catch and hold that spirit close, guarded with our love of humanity and the earth.

This is why I write.

Elizabeth Maxwell-Batten

"Art is the stored honey of the human soul,

gathered on wings of misery and travail".

Theodore Dreiser

Cowslips

(This is another stirring poem by my mother)

"Somehow the field was private,

Not private with a notice –

It was private private with beautifulness.

The cowslips could be seen through the gate;

It was only a simple field gate in the early morning stillness.

A missel thrush sang in the hedgerows.

I took my shoes off,

to walk over the field in shoes would be sacrilege.

The dew was still cold, no sun yet.

I picked wild .cowslips.

One here, one there,

I buried my face in the sweet soothing flowers.

I felt thankful.

When I carried them home,

I stopped at an old lady's cottage,

"here are some flowers" I said –

Her face lit up,

As she held them gently.

But that was years and years ago

when I was a child.

I can't find any cowslips now."

By Elizabeth Maxwell-Batten

Mum may have felt somewhat spiritually or emotionally alone in life while not easily able to share her thoughts outwardly. Voicing feelings into a poetic expression was possibly her way to communicate inner aches, joys, desires and a hunger to reach out for something sacred in our human journey.

I Miss Her

(A Poem by my sister – for our Mother)

I thought I missed the blue in her eyes,

then I looked up at the sky.

I thought I missed her gentle voice,

then I heard the breeze in the trees.

I thought I missed her soft smiling face,

until I looked into the center of a flower that was in

full bloom.

I thought I missed her lovely smell,

until I knelt down and smelt the buttercups growing

wild in the field.

I thought I missed her gentle touch,

until soft heather touched my cheek

With love From Margherita (Bo)

My sister.

Forty Years Later

Sitting on one of the wooden benches along the 'Goat Walk' as it is fondly called in Topsham and looking musingly across the estuary to the other side, I wondered how my life would unfold. What events would take place, how many children would I have and as most young girls contemplated - when would true and undying love enter my life? I was seventeen years old.

Now sitting on the same wooden bench gazing out at the unchanged view, I was at this moment looking back at life; the life that *had* actually unfolded for me. The same solace enveloped me now while sitting on that bench as had done forty years earlier. This time I was a little weather beaten and weary of life's storms, but still grateful to be breathing the calm evening air. The youthful wonder, apprehension, fear, hope and excitement of forty years earlier had dissipated over time – replaced by inevitable maturity and sporadic acceptance.

I didn't become a ballet dancer, *but* I danced! I didn't raise children, but I gave birth to a beautiful daughter and found creativity in my own way. Some beloved dogs in my life gave me the opportunity to wholly love and be loved. I didn't accumulate wealth but I *have* felt rich on a few occasions. Marriage and divorce seemed a fated part of my emotional and spiritual growth.

Whatever contrasting ideas and plans I may have had, *this* is the life that was given to me and now I was looking back as though seeing a painting. Not sure though whether I had been the artist or whether a greater hand equipped with easel and paintbrush had created our shared human design. Was my life a painting in itself, or was I merely part of a bigger picture – where separate lives intermingled harmoniously or clashed dramatically in a consequential way. Will we ever know the answers to such philosophical questions?

Do any of us look back with full satisfaction on the life we have lived? If truth be told, are we as mere mortals in control of events and do we really have choices? Sitting on that bench and breathing in the tranquil whisper of existence, I recognized that there is one choice I *do* have, and that is to find it in my heart to love and value this life and the whole of existence, however it may have unfolded.

Entrance to 'The Goat Walk' in Topsham

The Goat walk in Topsham

Epilogue

This picture of the *Bridge Inn*, with its big fireplace and notable charm is a familiar sight in Topsham and brings back memories of cheery visits. The Queen went to see this historic landmark in 2003. Topsham residents' have their pint of *Old Peculiar* brew, while sitting on the aged stone wall overlooking a beautiful wide river running through the green fields of Devon.

My stories about life in England are seen from the point of view of a Brit as well as someone looking through the eyes of other cultures.

Switzerland, America, India and Thailand have affected me in remarkable ways. Immersed in the traditions of varying countries, one naturally integrates them all. Though my own roots are ultimately and deeply embedded in England, anywhere that feels like home causes our human heart to sing with reassurance, and I feel at home in most places.

Whenever I return to England I am beset with excitement; the spring flowers emanating their beautiful scents, my much-loved siblings and our Jack Russell dogs - are all incentives that will always lure me back to my roots.

I'm cheerfully at ease in the warm and intoxicating Hawaiian Islands where fragrances and colors flourish in abundance; I feel happy in the pure crisp mountains of Alaska and equally comfortable amongst the magnificent desert hills of Arizona. There is a familiar and welcoming sense of joy whenever I visit Zurich Switzerland and I am familiarized with the dramatically different nuances of India, a land filled with history and mysticism. Most recently my home in the city of San Antonio, Texas has introduced a warm hearted Hispanic culture into my life – and reminds me of my mother's delicious Mexican rice dishes.

If *'home is where the heart is'* - then my heart is in all these places.

"In the heart of each, I hear the music of all"

"We are all part of the Universe,

so its story, is our story"

Brian Edward Cox.
Physicist and Humanist

Photo by Ritzy Ryciak

Charmiene Maxwell-Batten was born in Devon, England in the small town of Axminster. At six weeks old she left for Uganda, with her parents and brother Jonathan. Charmiene's father was a government inspector and consultant in the coffee industry on the East African continent. Charmiene and her brother lived in Kampala for ten years as the family grew; those were joyful events when Justin and Margherita were born at Entebbe hospital in Kampala. Later when the family returned to England, Dominic our youngest sibling was born in Dorset.

Charmiene has a profound interest in natural health, alternative medicine, herbal remedies as well as an early and creative passion for ballet and writing, which has continued throughout her life.

Her many years in Switzerland, India, Thailand and USA have provided a deep appreciation for cultural diversity and her visits to three spiritual teachers in India have given her an understanding of our inner and human journey in this world. In 1992 she was inspired to write and share her experiences.

Charmiene's paternal great grandfather, Reverend Sabine Baring-Gould, the author of the well-known hymns *'Onward Christian Soldiers'* and *'Now the Day is Over'*, was also an avid traveler and major literary figure, who was an authority on myths, legends and folklore. Baring-Gould was a friend and literary peer of George Bernard Shaw and Arthur Conan Doyle. His marriage to Grace Taylor was the basis of the character Eliza Doolittle in Pygmalion. Rumor has it that that his estate Lew Trenchard Manor in Dartmoor, provided the atmosphere and setting for Conan Doyle's *'Hound of the Baskervilles'*. Baring Gould also appears as a character in Laurie King's Sherlock Holmes novel – *'The Moor'*.

Sabine Baring-Gould

Charmiene at Lew Trenchard Manor in 1983

Charmiene at Lew Trenchard Manor

210

Beautiful Dartmoor

"Do you see how every little breath of wind that sighed against the shore, was written down? The record of the weeping skies is brought to light; and now that which was hidden is revealed. He who has written these down on tables of stone, must have recorded the tears which fall on the earth and which to many, are unknown"

Sabine Baring-Gould

From his book 'The Mystery of Suffering'

I wonder whether my great grandfather felt lonely and often misunderstood – as I read his books written over a century ago, I'm profoundly touched by his expression of insight and awareness. I even wonder if today he is fully appreciated for all his written work.

Besides the acclaim for having written the hymn *'Onward Christian Soldiers'* – his capacity for depth and understanding should stir the consciousness and soul of any spiritual seeker today.

Charmiene Maxwell-Batten

215

218